COSMIC SECRETS OF THE MASTERS OF WISDOM:

A FINAL SOLUTION TO WORLD PROBLEMS

Plus:
The Magick of the Pentagram Revealed

William Alexander Oribello

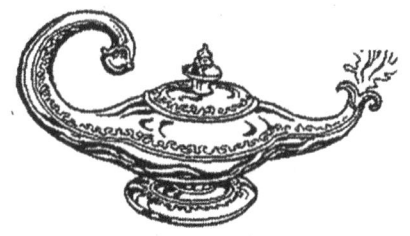

INNER LIGHT PUBLICATIONS

COSMIC SECRETS OF THE MASTERS OF WISDOM

William Alexander Oribello

**ALL RIGHTS RESERVED
COPYRIGHT © 2009
INNER LIGHT**

ISBN 1 60611 063 2
EAN 978 1 60611 063 8

Science/New Age/Occult Technology

No part of this book may be reproduced, stored in a retrieval system Or transmitted in any form or by any means, electronic, mechanical, photocopying, or recording, without permission of the publisher.

Timothy Green Beckley, Editor Director
Carol Rodriguez, Cover Art
Tim Swartz, Sean Casteel Assistant Editors

Free catalog from Inner Light Publications
Box 753, New Brunswick, NJ 08903

Visit our website at:
www.conspiracyjournal.com

THE FINAL SOLUTION

CONTENTS

INHABITANTS OF THE UNIVERSE....................1

MAN, THE GREAT MYSTERY........................8

LEGIONS OF DARKNESS EXPOSED..................26

LEGIONS OF LIGHT REVEALED....................33

MYSTIC LIGHT COMMUNICATIONS..................50

COPYRIGHT 1985 BY WILLIAM ALEXANDER ORIBELLO
ALL RIGHTS RESERVED. NO PORTION OF THIS WORK
MAY BE REPRODUCED IN ANY FORM WITHOUT WRITTEN
PERMISSION OF THE PUBLISHER

PLEASE NOTE. . .

THE AUTHOR SHARES THE CONTENTS OF THIS WORK
FOR WHATEVER SPIRITUAL OR LITERARY VALUE IT
MAY BE TO THE READER. NO CLAIMS OF SUPERNATURAL
THERAPUTIC, MEDICAL, COSMETIC OR ANY OTHER
EFFECTS ARE MADE OR SHOULD BE IMPLIED. NO
RESPONSIBILITY IS ASSUMED BY THE AUTHOR, PUBLISHER
OR VENDOR FOR THE OUTCOME OF ANY EXPERIMENTATION
WITH THE INFORMATION CONTAINED IN THIS MANUSCRIPT.

**INNER LIGHT PUBLICATIONS
BOX 753
NEW BRUNSWICK, N.J. 08903**

I dedicate this work to the Cosmic Hierarchy of Ascended Masters and Space Brothers who have lovingly helped me throughout my life. I also wish to thank my good friend Wm. K. Flaherty who shared his ideas on the levels of human evolution, which I have used with my own concepts in chapter two. Last, but not least, I acknowledge my publisher Timothy Green Beckley who has been a constant source of encouragement and help in releasing my books to the world in this New Age.

William Alexander Oribello,
The Mystic Light Society,

CHAPTER 1-INHABITANTS OF THE UNIVERSE

"In the beginning God created the heaven and the earth. And the earth was without form, and void; and darkness was upon the face of the deep. and the Spirit of God moved upon the face of the waters."

Genesis 1: 1,2.

The first four words of this passage of scripture states, "In the beginning God." These words reveal the existence of a supreme being before and at the time of the creation, for this being is the intelligent force which creates and sustains all manifestation.

This first scripture of the Holy Bible implies that the work of creation was a completed work. However, in the next verse we read, "And the earth was without form, and void; and darkness was upon the face of the deep. And the Spirit of God moved upon the face of the waters." The greatest of Bible Scholers have been puzzled by this statement for if God created all things at one instant, why was it without form at another instant?

The answer is found in mystic symbolism: In the beginning God created the heaven and the earth as a concrete idea, as a finished thought. In mystic symbolism, heaven may implicate a finer frequency of matter, and earth a denser manifestation of matter. But all these things were created as a finished thought first, then manifested as form later. Thus we have the words, "and the earth was without form", which means that dense matter had not yet taken form. Darkness on the face of the deep implies

space which was void of living manifestation. Therefore, God formed a thought of the completed creation of the cosmos, but the thought was shrouded in the inactivity of non-manifestation or darkness. Then the Spirit of God moved upon the face of the waters. This means that God imparted life giving motion to his thought.

Darkness is the absence of light and the creative thought of God could not take form until light projected it into living action and existence. The first recorded words of God were "Let there be light." Genesis 1:3.

THE PRIMORDIAL LIGHT:

According to this scripture, when God spoke light into being, the Sun, Moon and Stars were not yet created. The light which God spoke into existence has been called the Primordial Light by mystics of all ages. This is because it was a medium of action through which all things came into living manifestation. Light is the medium though which our sense of sight operates, for no matter how well we see, sight is impossible without light.

St. John the Evangelist said, "God is Light" (I John 5:1.) Therefore, when God created the Primordial Light he projected himself into his creation giving it life and form. Light is a vibration which is transmitted at a velocity of 186,300 miles per second. A wise teacher opened my understanding to the following illustration: On a motion picture film are thousands of still photographs. If we place the film on a projector and set up a screen, a modern day miracle takes place; the pictures on the film seem to come alive on the screen. The agent which gives motion to the pictures is the projector. But the agent which gives life to the pictures is the light.

God is light and God projected himself into his thought and manifested a living creation. Science calls this the Great explosion which resulted in the material universe.

THE MANIFESTATION OF GOD:

At the dawn of a new day of creation, the Great Spirit was, and existed from all eternity to boundless eternity. It was both male and female, yet neither; It was in all space, yet occupied no space; This was pure spirit, without known form or limitation, it was the true Almighty God.

The true God condensated himself into spiritual form and manifestation which could be known as inspired revelation to the spiritually aware humans which would live at a later time. The Manifestation of God is tenfold and reveals itself to us as ten divine names of power, which are among other numerous divine names. They are:
1. Eheieh, which means the crown and "I Am";
2. Jehovah, which means divine wisdom and essence;
3. Jehovah Elohim, which means Lord God of Understanding;
4. El, which means the Merciful Creator;
5. Elohim Gibor, which means the Potent One;
6. Eloah Vadaath, which means the Strong and Beautiful One;
7. Jehovah Tzaboath, which means the Victorious God of Hosts;
8. Elohim Tzaboath, which means the Glorious God of Hosts;
9. Shaddai El Chai, which means the Omnipotent God of the Foundation;
10. Adonai Melekh, which means the Almighty Ruler of The Kingdom.

These ten names and manifestations of God form the descending scale by which God manifested himself. This is known to teachers of the secret tradition known as the Kabbalah as the Tree of Life. From the first ten emanations of God, the Great Spirit created the ten levels which form the hierarchy of Archangels. They are:

1. Metatron, which means the Angel of the Presence;
2. Raziel, which means Teacher of the Mysteries;
3. Tsapkiel, which means Teacher of Contemplation;
4. Tzadkiel, which means Angel of Justice;
5. Samael, which means Angel of Judgement;
6. Michael, which means Captain of the Lord's Host;
7. Haniel, which means the Angel of Grace;
8. Raphael, which means the Angel of Healing;
9. Gabriel, which means Helper of the Divine Man;
10. Sandalphon, which means The Deliverer.

These mighty Archangels rule over the hierarchy of Angels which form a chain of forces within the levels of existence to help humanity. The ten levels of Angelic Hosts rule over a multitude of lesser spirits which aid them in their work in ministering to the creation of God. They are:

1. Chaioth Ha Kadosh, which means the Supreme Cherubim;
2. Orphanim, which means Living Creatures of the Wheels;
3. Aralim, which means Thrones of the Mighty;
4. Chash Malim, which mean Angels of Light;
5. Seraphim, which means the Fiery Serpents of Light;
6. Malachim, which means the Rulers;
7. Elohim, which means the Principalities;
8. Ben Elohim, which means the Sons of God;
9. Cherubim, which mean Ministering Angels;
10. Ishim, which means the Cosmic Hierarchy.

NATURE'S FINER FORCES:

The condensation of the Divine Essence into the material universe reveals a host of spirits involved in sustaining physical manifestation. There are ten types of spirits with lesser spirits under their command. The spirits of nature's finer forces may be considered as lesser angels which manifest, not as pure spirit or astral matter, but as ultra-fine physical matter or ether. Therefore, they are not commonly visible to the naked eye. Science has recently proven what mystics have taught for ages: that there are manifestations of physical matter so fine in frequency so as to not be perceivable to our physical senses. The ten types of beings which compose the hierarchy of the finer forces of nature are as follows:

1. Rashith Ha Galagalum, which means the Premium Mobile or Keepers of the Life Force;
2. Masloth, which means the Rulers of The Zodiac;
3. Shabbathai, which means the Ruling influence of Saturn;
4. Tzedeg, Which means the Ruling Influence of Jupiter;
5. Madim, which means the Ruling Influence of Mars;
6. Shemesh, which means the Ruling Influence of the Sun;
7. Nogah, which means the Ruling Influence of Venus;
8. Kokab, which means the Ruling Influence of Mercury;
9. Levanah, which means the Ruling Influence of the Moon;
10. Cholom Yosodoth, which means the Kingdom of the Elements or Hierarchy of Nature Spirits which sustain the Four Physical Elements.

The four levels of God's manifested creation that we have just considered contain a descending scale of involution by which spirit energy expresses itself from the World of Spirit to our level of existence. However, in our realm there is a duality of forces as we will now reveal.

FORCES OF DARKNESS:

Within our physical realm of existence there are legions of spirits who have fallen from the exhalted state into a career of influencing humankind in a negative way, attempting to keep them in ignorance of spiritual truth and the path of genuine occultism. There are ten rulers of these evil forces which St. Paul described in the following scripture:

> "For we wrestle not against flesh and blood, but against principalities, against powers, against the rulers of the darkness of this world, against spiritual wickedness in high places."
>
> Ephesians 6:12

Each of these rulers has legions of corrupt spirits under his command. The ten rulers of darkness are as follows:
1. Thaumiel-Lucifer, which means satan or adversary;
2. Adam Belial, which means teacher of corruption;
3. Satharial, which means one who conceals God's truth;
4. Gamchicoth, which means the sower of discord;
5. Golab, which means the flaming anger;
6. Togarini, which means the snare or one who entraps;
7. Baal, which means the messenger of darkness;
8. Adramelek, which means one who inspires gossip;
9. Lileth, which means the degrading obscenity;
10. Nahemoth, which means impurity.

We shall consider the rulers of light and darkness in more detail, along with methods of dealing with them, later in this present work.

The different levels of existence that we have just considered has been depicted in many types of symbols.

Such a symbol is the one which appears to the right. This has been called the Alchemist's Tree of Life.

This symbol reveals the levels of existence as layers of symbolic pictures. The Hebrew mystic teachings, known as the Cabballa has a similar symbol that consisted of ten circles connected by twenty two lines. This was called the Cabballistic Tree of Life.

Meditation upon such symbols is believed to bring about a spiritual awakening in the observer.

CHAPTER 2-MAN, THE GREAT MYSTERY

Man is more than just a physical being. Man is a living spirit, and a living soul which sets each individual apart as a one of a kind entity, yet part of every other soul in creation. The ancient teachers of wisdom advised their students to "Know Thyself". If you will attempt to know yourself completely from the outer physical shell to the very core of your being, then you hold the key which unlocks the door to understanding life's mysteries.

All things, at all levels of existence is composed of the same substance which is spirit. The difference between the different levels of existence and their manifold manifestations is the degree of vibration in which they manifest. Spirit energy permeates all things, even that which seems to be nothing.

THE LIVING MIRACLE:

Multiplied billions of atoms bind together by the powerful divine creative force to form molecules and finally cells which form the hair, flesh, blood and bone which become the great masterpiece called man.

Within the chest is the most efficient pump ever made. It begins to pulsate and move blood through the developing tissues months before birth, and it continues to function throughout life. This outstanding pump is the human heart. At the time of birth the heart weighs about one ounce and is 1 ½ inches in diameter. By adulthood the heart weighs about one pound and and is as large as your fist. The male heartbeat rate is 68 to 76 beats per

minute. The female heartbeat rate is 74 to 80 beats per minute. Let's take for an example an average heartbeat of 75 per minute; that figures out to be 4,500 beats an hour, 108,000 beats a day, 39,420,000 beats a year. Imagine how many times a heart beats in a lifetime.

The human skeleton is made up of about 206 bones. Fifty percent of bone is calcium combined with phosphate. The development and formation of bones are controlled by harmones, vitamins and minerals.

The nervous system integrates the activities of all parts of the body. The central nervous system is made up of the brain and spinal cord. The sensations of hearing, tasting, smelling, touching and seeing are experienced in the brain. The brain translates the messages from the sensory fibers into sensations and directs impulsive response. The spinal cord controls reflex activity.

THE CONSTITUTION OF MAN:

The three dimensional physical body is just one of several components of the whole person. Man possesses an additional physical body (which we will consider in a moment), an astral body, a mental body and a spiritual body. These various bodies are used by the True Self or Spirit of Man to function within the different levels of existence .

The dense physical body is made of solids, liquids and gases which form the manifestation of physical matter. However, there is a higher form of physical life which has been termed "Ether" and this is the substance from which the higher physical body is composed. This vehicle has been called "the Etheric Double"

"the Vital Body" and by other terms. This body harnesses and distributes life-force and vitality to every part of the lower physical body. The Vital Body has seven energy centers termed "Chakras", through which it distributes the life-force into the physical body via the seven ductless glands.

THE ASTRAL BODY:

Beyond our physical world, there exists a fourth dimensional plane of existence called "the Astral World". This is the plane of forces where emotion, desire and other feelings originate and develop to form levels of expression, from the lowest hell to the highest heaven possible on this plane. While the physical body sleeps, man travels to this dimension clothed in the astral body. However, the memory of such experiences usually vanishes when man dreams during the few moments before awakening.

After physical death, most people dwell on the astral realm unless they have evolved beyond the emotional stage while in physical life. There are places of gross negative vibration in the astral world which may appear to a visionary as the traditional Hell and purgatory. Other areas may appear to be exact replicas of cities on earth. And there are even finer levels of the astral which has been termed "the Summerland" or "Paradise". A person is attracted to the level of the astral which corresponds to his evolvement at the time of physical death. If a person ends up in an undesirable place it is not so much a matter of divine punishment which has sent them there-it is their own level of vibration which causes them suffering until they have realized the error of their feelings and raise their vibration into a higher level of expression. When this is accomplished an angel, spirit guide or the spirit of a loved one will guide the repentant soul to a better place within the astral realm.

The development of the astral body depends on how we refine our emotions. It is wise to observe how we feel about people and situations and attempt to transform all negative emotions into positive ones. there are a number of ways to do this. For example, if we feel upset at someone and the feeling is eating away at us we could clear the air in the following manner: Write a letter to the person, stating every detail of your ill feelings towards them. There are some things that are better left unsaid to the person face to face. This is because some words can hurt a relationship permenantly. Therefore, this letter writing technique is very effective. Remember that you are writing out your anger, not verbalizing it, so let your feelings express freely. At the end of the letter write a positive sentence to the effect that with God's help you forgive the person. The final act is to burn the letter. This burning ritual is symbolic of the fact that you are transforming your negative feelings of anger, envy, annoyance, jealousy, hurt or any other ill feelings into higher expressions of understanding and forgiveness. You can use this method about anything that troubles you, and you should try this first and avoid personal confrontations if at all possible. You may have to repeat this exercise more than once for best results.

THE MENTAL BODY:

The mental world is the realm from which all thought activities originate. I must add that the thought activities I refer to are not the mundane thoughts which most people experience, but the deep contemplative and higher philosophical thoughts of the true thinker. The mental world may be considered to be divided into a lower and higher region. The lower region is termed the World of Concrete Thought. The higher region is termed the World of Causal or Abstract Thought. The mental world is a dimension of more advanced beings, beyond the astral vibration.

Man possesses a mental body which is the medium of thought energy in his experience. This mental body must be developed in order for a person to transcend the limitations of human existence. This is accomplished by constant effort towards the goal of self-improvement, and development of the mental faculties by reading and application of mind training and meditation techniques.

THE SPIRITUAL BODY:

Many sparks issue from a flame. The Great Spirit may be contemplated to be a great fire, and the true spiritual beings of men may be compared to the sparks. From the Cosmic World of God there issued a denser frequency of existence termed the Spiritual World. Man possesses a spiritual body which vibrates in harmony with this realm of spirit. However, most people are not aware of this spiritual body and it is therefore in a dormant state.

In the higher spiritual work as taught in this book, you may awaken this Spiritual Body by attunement with the great ascended beings and, above all, by raising your consciousness into greater levels of awareness.

LEVELS OF HUMANS:

There are several levels of human evolution. However, before we consider these I wish to point out that a person does not have to remain in a certain condition or method of behavior. A person can change and improve his or her life. All it takes is a firm determination to do so, and the ability to remain on the path of mystical studies. To just continue in teachings such as this will uplift a person's consciousness into greater levels of unfolding wisdom and beauty which comes from the True Self.

The 1st. Level of Humans may be described as those who are egotistical, cruel, selfish, hateful, greedy, insensitive, and any other type of closed minded trait you can imagine. The positive aspects of their behavior is that they are hard workers and have an interest in their own families.

The 2nd. Level are those who use their cunning to get what they want at the expense of others. They are closed minded and hostile to the views and opinions of others. Such persons lack genuine interest in true spiritual development, and participate in such activities only as a means to use others, or to rule over weaker persons. They may have a strict moral code which they tend to impose upon those around them, making no concessions except when they wish to break the code, thus leading a double life. The positive aspects of this level is that they can be industrious and be active in community affairs.

The 3rd. Level souls can be very proud to the point of being judgmental and blaming others for their own mistakes. They are generally unstable in work or commitment. Their positive aspects tend towards religious and reform activities, but these are colored with prejudice or disregard for others who may not agree with their own beliefs. They can be artistic and intellectually conscious. The more advanced on this level can be kind and generous. They are hard workers and good organizers.

The 4th. Level souls represent the first great step into higher consciousness. Therefore, we will begin with their positive traits and also reveal how they can fall into negative patterns if they are not following the master plan in their lives. These people are sincere, compassionate, adventurous, generous and good leaders. They have high spiritual values and seek to help

others. They are tolerant of the religious views of others that may not be in agreement with their own, and realize that truth may have many shades of awareness. They are optimistic and adapt well to changes in their life. When a person of this level begins to awaken to their true potential they may realize that they are incompatable with their marriage partner or companion. This may cause them to seek relationships outside the home, and many have found their true Soul-Mate in this manner. If a 4th. Level Soul has not come into their true awareness they can be very unhappy people and tend to fall into negative traits such as frequent emotional stress, impatience, insecurity, over sensitivity and difficulty in understanding the self.

The 5th. Level Soul is one who is on his or her way out of the illusions of the lower dimensions, and on their way into a genuine relationship with God. They have great inner awareness, kindness and understanding towards others, great counseling talents, outstanding patience and generosity towards all forms of life. This great soul has evolved to the point of being able to inspire others towards higher metaphysical consciousness. They may find another person on the path with whom they can share their expressions of the finer forms of love, and this can be manifested as a story book love affair come true. A level 5 soul who has not realized their true nature may fall into the following negative traits: Over-reactive sensitivity, wasting time and energy, avoiding material duties, isolation problems and a general disgust or indifference to life. Even those who have been awakened can fall back into some of these negative traits from time to time when they become too burdened by negative surroundings or traumatic experiences. Therefore, this soul should walk softly and pace their worldly activities. A person of this level at best when a totally optimistic outlook is maintained.

The 6th. Level Soul is one who has transcended the need to reincarnate into physical life. They have overcome over half of their karma, meaning that they have worked it out by experience, application of cosmic law and selfless service to others. Therefore, this soul is permitted to work out the balance of their karma from the mental realm of existence, and act as guides to aspiring souls on the path. Such are known as Masters of the Wisdom. Those of this evolution who still walk among us are termed unascended masters; while those who have passed out from this life are known as the Ascended Masters of the Wisdom. This is because they have ascended from bondage to the wheel of birth, death and rebirth. I must also add that this type of soul has overcome the negative astral emotions to such a degree as to transmute their astral bodies into the finer essence of spiritual mentality.

The 7th. Level Soul is one who has worked out all of their karmic debts and have ascended into the spiritual realm. They are often called the Lords of Karma and they are in charge of souls on the lower scale of evolution. These souls are aware of their entire past and have full access to the records which contain the accounts of all events and lives, known as the Akashic Records.

OUR PLACE IN ETERNITY:

We are told, from a religious standpoint, that we have but one life in which to perfect ourselves and that afterwards we will go to one of two places: If we have lived a good life (according to the religion's standards) we go to heaven. If we were evil we go to a place called hell.

On one hand we are given a clear cut philosophy of how it is

supposed to be and are admonished to keep a certain moral code, and a simple faith. On the other hand we observe that it is not quite that simple. We look around us and see that life has not equally shared its opportunities with all.

We are taught that God is just and good, yet we see many inequalities among our fellow humans. If, indeed, we only have one life in which to prepare for eternal bliss or eternal pain, then why are not all given an equal chance to do so? The inequalities of life are the cold hard facts which any thinking person notices and admits to.

Many people, upon noticing things, find themselves on the razor's edge and begin to question even the existence of any God at all. Some will come to the conclusion that even if there is a God, he is certainly not fair to allow such unjust conditions as life has distributed to many.

The fact of the matter is that God is just and good. However, God has established certain universal laws which work the same for all, and are totally impersonal. These laws, when kept, bring well being to the keeper. On the other hand, when neglected and broken, these laws bring retribution to the one in violation of them. It is not so much a matter of reward and punishment, but rather a matter of each person attracting to themselves that which they are and that which they have done.

We can easily understand life when we discover and accept the teaching of Reincarnation. There has been a wide acceptance of this belief in the past several years. One reason for this is the fact that it makes sense-more sense than the dogmatic belief that we have only one life in which to justify or condemn our soul.

There are, however, some misunderstandings about the teaching of reincarnation which I will try to clear up now; One thing which puzzles a thinking person is the question, "Why must a person return to physical life to learn the lessons which may be better taught at higher levels of existence?" My answer to that question is this: We learn according to the limitation or expansion of our consciousness. In most people, consciousness is limited to the physical level of existence. The average living person cannot comprehend any thing beyond this life in a genuine form of realization. Therefore, to such people, lessons are best learned in this physical realm. For example, if we cause a certain type of pain to another which could be avoided, we cannot fully comprehend what we have done until it is done to us. If we have deprived others of certain things or pleasures of life, then we must also be deprived in order to fully realize how it feels, and that is only possible if we experience the return of our actions at the same level in which we acted towards others. This has been called "Karma" or "the Law of Compensation". In every one of us there is that inner voice which warns us not to do certain things, and lets us know when we fail. If we learn to listen to our inner voice we will be well on our way to attainment

WHY ARE WE HERE?

Another question one may ask is, "Why can't we receive all of our rewards and punishments here and now?" The answer to that is contained in one word-"Mercy". We have enough to be concerned about just with the daily neccessities of life. If we got back all the retribution of our actions in one lifetime we could not bear it. We see by this that the Law of Compensation (Karma) is merciful and just to allow us to work out our debts over a period of time.

One of the most perplexing questions concerning reincarnation

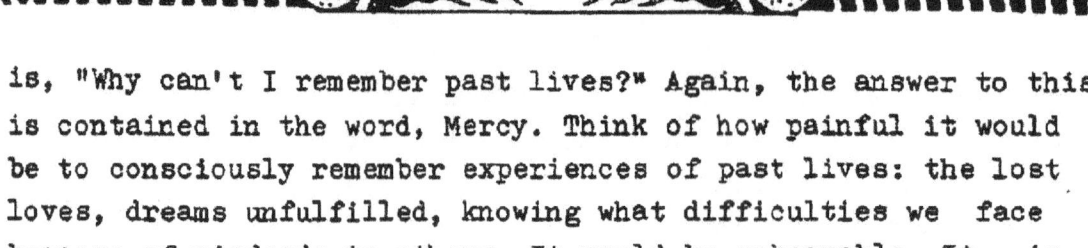

is, "Why can't I remember past lives?" Again, the answer to this is contained in the word, Mercy. Think of how painful it would be to consciously remember experiences of past lives: the lost loves, dreams unfulfilled, knowing what difficulties we face because of misdeeds to others. It would be unbearable. It is difficult enough to brood over yesterday's mistakes.

ONE LIFE-MANY BIRTHS:

In ancient India the concept of "One life-many births" was taught. By considering this concept we come to the realization that our life is one. It is not that we have had many lives; we have only one life, one existence that we have expressed through a number of births and deaths. The reason for it all is to gain experience.

A wise man told me that by considering a string of light bulbs, this truth would become apparent. It was during the festivities of a Christmas Season that I admired a string of multicolored Christmas Tree lights. There was something about them that prompted me to further meditation on the matter. Then I was told that there were several bulbs of different colors, but the current of electrical power and the wire which linked the bulbs were one source of energy which activated the bulbs. One could break one or several bulbs but the remaining ones would still light up. Think about that.

HOW MANY RETURNS?:

Now we come to the next important question: "How many times must I return?" In answer to your question I will first call your attention to the scripture in the Holy Bible which says, " The sins of the fathers are visited upon the children to the third and fourth generation." Exodus 20:5. Now, this does not mean

that children suffer for the sins of their forefathers as it is commonly believed. What it does mean is that we ourselves may reap the harvest of negative seeds which we have planted by our misdeeds up to three or four lifetimes ago.

This leads us to the conclusion that we have at least three or four lifetimes here. I must make clear, however, that we cannot limit our thinking in such matters of universal importance as rebirth. I believe that some of us have been here hundreds of times for specific reasons. Meditation on these things will bring greater understanding.

Progress is the key word of this present lesson. As long as our consciousness is limited to physical life as experienced on this planet or others like it, then are we bound to return here in order to gain more experience. The purpose of this experience is to afford us ample opportunity to search for, discover and apply the higher concepts which will free us.

THE BEGINNING OF FREEDOM:
We must not limit ourselves to think that this planet is the only place of physical existence. There are many living planets throughout the universe; some with a more advanced way of life than we have here. Our experience in physical rebirth may progress to other planets besides Earth.

As stated earlier, as long as our consciousness is limited to this physical existence, then must we return until we learn our lessons well. On the other hand, when our consciousness has expanded into other dimensions, we can benefit from the vibration of those dimensions.

You may find, upon meeting a certain person, that you have an intense dislike for the person. The reason for this is that either that person's vibration of thought is so out of harmony with yours, or you had some undesirable experience with that person in another lifetime. They could be a past lover with whom you had a falling out, or even an old enemy. The reason that you would meet such a person again is to work things out between the two of you. It should be our goal to remove all negative vibrations from our lives by forgiving all who have harmed us from all lifetimes. We should also ask forgiveness from all people we have harmed, past and present. It would be impossible to personally face all the people we have known in this life, let alone all past lives, here and now. However, there is one thing we can do here and now which will free us from the need to return and face them at some future time: we can communicate with them at a cosmic level by forgiving and asking forgiveness while we are in a state of prayer and meditation. You do not have to consciously remember everyone, just make a mental or emotional verbal statement to the effect that you forgive and release all persons who have harmed you, and this you do from your heart as God is your helper. You would also reach out and ask forgiveness from all persons that you have harmed, in this and other lifetimes. When we free ourselves from the mental causes of Karma we then become free and break away from the wheel of illusion.

Love is the means which expands our consciousness and leads us to liberation. When Jesus taught the people to love their enemies it was more than just a religious concept: it was, and is, the scientific application of a great path to liberation. The more we study and meditate on such knowledge as presented in this lesson, the more understanding we become of others, and of life in general.

It is the same when you meet a stranger yet feel a love and harmony towards that person. It may be an old love or friend crossing your path again so that the both of you can become more enriched.

Several people have asked me how long of a time elapses between incarnations. There is really no time limit. A person may spend a thousand years in the beyond before returning or may return in a few months, or years. This depends on several things, among which are, the neccessity of working things out to bring liberation, or to fulfill some special purpose.

There are a group of advanced spirits known as the Guardians, or "Lords of Karma". These beings are in charge of us and they see to it that we are reborn in the surroundings which will afford us the means to correct our mistakes and evolve.

Some students have asked if knowledge of past lives is beneficial. The answer to this is found in a quotation of a great man which says, "Only by knowing the past can the future be judged".

Knowledge of past lives can be of help to us. However, I must remind the student that the absence of this memory is a blessing. It would be most unbearable to come into a new life with full knowledge of past mistakes, and to know what trials are ahead for us. Life is better lived one day at a time.

As a person develops into higher awareness they do get what are termed "flashbacks" of past lives. While we are falling asleep we may get scenes of people and places from past lives. This is because we are in a twilight state, as produced by deep meditation. This may also happen in our dreams. However, it may

also be events taking place in the Astral Realm as we do travel there during sleep, and at times we may begin to pick up on astral events even before going to sleep. The important thing to consider when seeking knowledge of past lives is what help such knowledge can give you in the present.

THE KEY OF KNOWLEDGE:

    The power to ascend the levels of the soul and thus free ourselves from the wheel of illusion lies within our ability to control our thinking. Everything we experience in our present existence begins in the realm of mind: when we entertain a thought (good or bad) long enough, it becomes a fixation until it condensates into the astral or emotional realm, and then finally manifests into our physical existence. Therefore, we may change our lives and create better conditions with thought.

    Your mind is a great and wonderful power within which controls your life in so many ways. The subconscious level of your mental awareness controls the unconscious or involuntary functions of the physical body, as well as stores all information you have received during your life. The conscious mind is the portion of your awareness which relates to everything around you through the medium of the five senses. It controls and directs the power of thought. It has the power to allow certain thoughts and impressions to pass through the gate of separation and into the subconscious storehouse, or to reject such impressions as are of a negative nature so that they do not become a fixation of consciousness. In reality, you do not have different minds, only different levels of awareness. It is an illusion to think that your mind is separate from other minds or from the Universal Mind (God); There is only one mind, and each individual is a portion of that one mind. You may ask, then why are some minds

evil in the nature of their thinking? The answer may be found
in the Biblical statement that we are made in the image of God:
Each one of us has been given the power to create our own world
of existence-to create our own heaven or hell by our thinking
and actions. God created with thought, manifestation of the
thought (action) and with the spoken word. We are each a microcosm of miniature universe. We create and control what we experience by our thoughts, words and actions. Any thought we give
energy to inspires us to action and expression through the spoken
word. This is why it is so important to maintain good or constructive thoughts, and reject negative or destructive ones. The reason
we have not fully realized the true nature of our thinking is
because our awareness has been clouded by illusions, generated
by negative spirits and people who walk the path of the fallen
and make it a practice to mislead other souls. When we awaken to
to who and what we really are we then realize that we can change
our lives by changing our thoughts.

> "...But be transformed by the renewing of your mind,
> that ye may prove what is that good, and acceptable,
> and perfect will of God
>
> Romans 12: 2

HOW THE MIND WORKS:

The conscious mind expresses what fears, prejudice, conditioned reactions and phobias have been stored in the subconscious
mind. As we receive outward impressions from people we meet or
situations around us, we react according to our programming. Thus
we realize that our conscious mind receives impressions from the
outside and reacts according to the degree of inner harmony or
conflict. You may see someone do a certain thing and react in
a way that may produce either a good or bad reaction, depending
on our inner preconceived ideas. Our consciousness will feel good

or bad regarding any situation or our dealing with any person according to how we have thought. This is why we must learn how to observe how we think about life and other people, and examine it in the light of justice and truth. If we do this honestly we will discover that we are changing for the better and becoming a truly beautiful person.

One type of situation which requires this self inventory is a love affair. When two people discover each other and fall in love they soon realize that problems arise because of their individual pasts. This is especially true if they are past the age of thirty. In such a case the persons had negative experiences with one or more other persons in the past, and this has created conditioned reactions to certain things words and situations. This creates undesirable conditions such as misunderstandings, arguments, fears, jealousy and resentment. They may judge their beloved just because they may say or do something which resembles another person from the past. This problem can be worked out when people realize that to live in the now is most important, and that we should consider each new person and situation we encounter as a new opportunity for happiness, rejecting any thought of past hurts which may ruin what can be a beautiful relationship. This practical philosophy applies to any type of situation as well as the one we have just considered.

Whatever is sustained in the mind becomes a feeling, and that feeling becomes an action. Therefore, we can truly change the course of our life by becoming more aware of what we allow to occupy our mind. In other words, by controlling the quality of our thoughts we can be sure of the feelings and actions which will follow. Every situation is created by the actions of someone, and those actions began with a thought.

Most humans dwell on thoughts which cause undesirable feelings and worries. Whatever we make a habit of thinking about becomes actual situations within our everyday life. A thought may be just a passing thought, but if we give it energy by constant dwelling on it, then we are nourishing it and thus creating its manifestation. If you wish to overcome negative conditions in your life and make your experience better, simply change your way of thinking. In other words, don't think about what you don't want. Give energy only to good thoughts and you will create good conditions and experiences for yourself. For every effect, there is a cause. Therefore, consider the fact that your thoughts are the cause of the effects, good or bad, within your life.

In this chapter on the mystery of man we have discovered several truths concerning the composition of man. However, the most important thing for us to consider is the power of thinking and its creative nature to affect our experience.

CHAPTER 3-LEGIONS OF DARKNESS EXPOSED

We are surrounded and influenced by many forces, both good and evil. We have the right and option to choose what influence becomes a part of our everyday life experience. However, we must keep in mind that we live in a world in which negative elements have the upper hand; this is because most people follow a negative pattern of thought, speech and action.

In the first chapter of this work I revealed how that the entities known as "fallen angels" form the distorted tree of life in this physical dimension. They inspire all negative thinking, speaking and action, of every description. It is this consciousness which influences the general thinking of the world. They do not work against any one individual, unless that person is a direct threat to the forces of darkness. Such a person would be a fervent worker for the advancement of God's Kingdom. If the person is making headway in personal development and influencing others for good, he or she may find that things may happen to discourage them from completion of their mission in life. The great founders of truth systems such as Jesus, Moses and others were targets of direct attack from these forces.

EARTHBOUND ENTITIES:

Earthbound entities are tormented souls of people who remain attached to certain things they have known in life, after they leave here through physical death. Not all earthbound souls are evil: some of them are confused individuals who refused to find the true meaning of life while alive. Others are too attached to things and people who remain a part of this physical existence.

I am not saying that it is wrong to care about things and people. What I am saying is that when we depart from this physical life we must release everything and everyone we have known to follow their own course and destiny, for we will then have to adjust to our new surroundings and responsibilities on the other side. An earthbound often wanders among the land of the living observing living persons doing the things they liked to do. This is a form of torment which they suffer, only because they have not released their hold on life and resolved their problems. Some earthbound souls are downright evil. They are the discarnate souls of people, who during life, were negative in their dealings with other people. When a person constantly thinks or feels negative, resentful, degenerative, spiteful or any other type of negation, that person will be in a very dark state of being after physical death unless they repent. These type of earthbounds observe living persons who may be weak or troubled and victimize such persons by implanting negative thoughts in the person's mind through mental telepathy. They take great pleasure in making people suffer and cause anxiety, arguments between couples, misunderstandings between friends and other things which cause heartache to living humans. They try to break down and possess a person so that they can use their body to perform horrible deeds to the point of murder or suicide in many cases. They frequent such places as taverns and areas of cities where negative vibrations run rampant, just waiting for the opportunity to pounce on vulnerable people. However, it is important that you understand that they do not just remain in such places; they may also be found wandering into ordinary homes and rural areas, always looking for a chance to poison someone with their negativity. When we realize such forces exist we can better arm ourselves against them and be more aware of the thoughts which pass through our mind.

THE SPIRIT OF ANTI-CHRIST:

There is a spirit which has been an influencing power in this world since the beginning of time. That spirit is the Spirit of The Christ that inspires the heart of man to seek the truth of who he is, where he came from and where he is going. However, there is another spirit which does battle against the Spirit of Christ. This other spirit has been called Anti-Christ. The anti-christ keeps the bulk of humanity in a cloud of misconception concerning the true nature of man and the cosmos. This spirit has also worked through many religions which corrupt the truth so as to rule over the masses with fear. True religion does not inspire people to worship God out of fear, but to ascend towards God through love and practice of the truth. The anti-christ is the very soul of Lucifer who led an entire race of spirits and angels into a rebellion which caused the fall of man, as describ- in the scriptures of all religions. In this period of time known as the New Age, the activities of the Christ and the anti-christ will increase to such a degree that the vibrations of this conflict will be felt by humankind with such intensity so as to bring about rapid changes in the world.

THE BROTHERHOOD OF DARKNESS:

The anti-christ holds sway over individuals who, although developed in certain mental powers, are negative in their nature and personality. Such persons are known as the Brotherhood of Darkness. Some members of this brotherhood are living persons who are in all types of occupations in all parts of the world. Others are discarnate spirits, many of whom are masters of the negative application of magic and mind power. The purpose of this brotherhood of darkness is to inspire humankind to follow a path of darkness. They thrive on negative emotions of hate, greed, lust and any other negative thing you can imagine. They gather the bulk of negative feelings, words, thoughts and deeds generated by humankind. They amplify the negation and send it back out on humanity. This is why we should try to generate only positive feelings, thoughts and actions. The world has already been burdened with an abundance of negativity and it seems that we are in a constant battle against the mental assaults of the Brotherhood of Darkness.

FALSE PROPHETS:

There are many charlatans who pose as ministers, spiritual workers and teachers of truth, but are in reality wolves in sheeps clothing. These false prophets dupe vulnerable people out of money and give only confusion and fear in return. The Brotherhood of Darkness inspire these people to misuse their gifts so that their victims lose faith in the true spiritual work. We must never judge the truth because of some false representative of truth. We can always recognize a false prophet by the fact that such persons seek to rule over others in some way; they use brainwashing techniques or fear to force people over to their way of thinking, or will not perform their services for those unable to pay their fees.

VAMPIRES:

There are some people who have degenerated to the point that they drain the life force from others. These have been called vampires. Living persons may be vampires when they constantly drain another person by taking too much of their time and energy rather than learn to stand on their own and develop. Some earthbound spirits become the type of vampires we read about in horror stories and see in movies. They prey on weak people, draining them of their energy and will power.

OVERCOMING THE LEGIONS OF DARKNESS:

We can overcome the forces of evil by maintaining a positive attitude and generating positive thoughts. As stated earlier in this work, our thoughts are the means by which we can change our life. The illustration below depicts the brave Knight in shining armour slaying the dragon and saving a lady in distress. This is symbolic of the conscious mind (the knight) keeping out negative thoughts (the dragon) to protect the subconscious mind (the woman in distress). We must reject all negative thoughts before they enter the subconscious and become a fixation.

Our thoughts, feelings and deeds can be the means to our freedom, or they can become the chains which bind us to a long earthbound existence after physical death. It is the quality of our expressions which determine our destiny.

The illustration to the right depicts an earthbound soul walking in darkness and bound by the chains of his undesirable deeds, thoughts and feelings which he failed to overcome during his physical life.

Such souls walk in the torments of their deeds and seek to inspire living humans to think, feel and live the way they had. They do this because some of them desire to bring others down to their level.

Some of the thoughts which torment us may be inspired by these degenerated spirits. When we are aware of this fact we can observe our thoughts with more wisdom and learn which to reject and which to admit into our consciousness. Everyone must walk the path of cleansing their inner self, sooner or later. Our conscious effort in this area will save us from many torments.

It can be a difficult task to overcome the negative thoughts which have beset us if we attempt to do it without the proper help. However, by entering a path of study with a genuine mystery school we can learn and master specific techniques which can help us find liberation from the limitations of our human existence.

Even after we enter the path we may find that it takes us a considerable time to overcome all of the negative thoughts, feelings and deeds of darkness. Only by constant effort will we become strong and powerful enough to change our life.

The illustration below depicts a demon with a bird in a nest on its head. This reveals a new meaning to the term "a little bird told me": Birds are often used as symbols for thoughts. Thus the bird in this illustration is symbolic of evil thoughts. The nest reveals that evil thoughts may find a nest, or resting place in our conscious and subconscious thinking. The demon is symbolic of the fact that we can become the devil or our own worse enemy by the thoughts we allow to dominate our thinking.

CHAPTER 4- LEGIONS OF LIGHT REVEALED

So far we have considered the finer forces of the cosmos and their manifestation in the world of matter, the nature of man with his multi-dimensional components, and the distortion of the universal energy as exemplified in the forces of darkness and their works. Now we will consider the all powerful group of souls who work in harmony with God. They are all powerful because good always overcomes evil. However, most humans are not aware of these Godly forces because they are too preoccupied with the negative aspects of life. In the first chapter we considered the levels of angels, now we will reveal the other levels of Light Workers and how they can assist humankind in their upward climb back to Godhood.

GOOD SPIRITS OF THE DEPARTED:

When a good person departs physical life they further their evolution by becoming a spirit guide to one or more persons who still live in this dimension. When I say "good person" I do not mean someone who was a strict religious person. Religion serves as a guide to lead us towards God consciousness. However, many of the precepts of religion are man made-not God made; they are only given in the name of God. Careful observation will reveal the truth of my statement. Any thinking person may realize that although each religion claims to have the correct teaching and path to heaven, there are truly sincere people in all religions. There are some people who do not claim any religion by practice, but live a life of true love and devotion to a higher concept of life. Such persons may be considered good. These precious souls are constantly evolving towards perfection on the Astral Plane and do so by serving those who need them here in physical life, for service is the true expression of love, and love is the path to God. The good spirits of the departed help us by implanting noble and inspirational thoughts in our minds, by trying to save us from danger or making bad mistakes, etc. They are ever present to help us if we allow them to do so. Your spirit guide may be one of your departed loved ones or an old friend-perhaps even someone you knew in a past life. At times a spirit guide evolves to an advanced degree or must reincarnate, and they must leave us, in which case another guide would be assigned to us. You may become familiar with your guide by attending a good metaphysical church or group, or by silent meditation and attempting mental contact. In my book "Sacred Magic" I reveal several truths about mediumship (communication with spirits).

THE CHRIST:

When the race of human spirits descended into dense matter the manifestation of God known as the Christ extended into this dimension for the purpose of reminding humankind of their own christ consciousness. Every inspiration we receive to seek the path back to our true origin comes from the Cosmic Christ. At times the Christ has manifested through advanced souls such as Jesus of Nazareth.

TEACHERS OF TRUE OCCULTISM:

The word Occult means hidden wisdom. However, most people associate that word with something negative because of dogmatic religious concepts. True occultism reveals how each human may attain to their true potential in life by the application of certain cosmic laws. This wisdom comes about when a person begins to discover themselves. True occultism is also called metaphysics.

Any teacher or minister who teaches metaphysical principles such as positive thinking, meditation or inner awareness is a true worker of God's Light for they lift man out of the depth of fear and limited consciousness, and inspire him to soar Godward without restriction.

REVELATIONS FROM OUTER SPACE:

There are some planets in the universe inhabited by advanced beings who have learned to live in peace and harmony with all forms of life. Some of these beings have advanced in science and technology to such a degree that they can travel to great distances within the universe in their special craft (commonly called Unidentified Flying Objects or U.F.O.s). The purpose of our brothers and sisters from space is to watch over us and others on planets which have not yet evolved to the point of living in harmony. These glorious beings have saved us from destruction many times, and have communicated with earthlings on numerous occaisions. One well known Space Brother is Ashtar. This powerful being has communicated with me at different times and I have printed his latest message in part two of this book in which are published the Mystic Light communications. Ashtar is the commander-in-chief of the free federation of planets, and is in charge of a large fleet of spaceships stationed above the Earth.

THE ROSY CROSS:

There have always been secret orders such as "Knights Templar", "Freemasons", "The Magi ", "Knights of the Round Table" and a host of others. One such order which has been well known for centuries is the Order of the Rosy Cross. The original order of the Rosy Cross was a school of Mystic Christianity according to its early publications. However, it is much more, because the true order of the Rosy Cross is not limited to any religious dogma or sect. It is a true society of Light in which all people of all religions and philosophies become one in a common purpose of discovering the power within nature, and being of service to others in the application of that power. Also, while there have been several physical organizations using the name Rosicrucian, the true order is not restricted to any one organization but manifests through any organization with a purpose sympathetic to its principles. The name Rosicrucian may be applied to any person who is a mystic, adept or master of an advanced degree and is in communion with an invisible body of Masters of Wisdom, of which I will reveal more in this chapter.

It is believed that the term Rosy Cross or Rosicrucian is derived from the name of its alledged founder, a man by the name of Christian Rosenkreuze. Its grand symbol is that of a rose on a cross or a rose on a heart. This latter symbol of a heart and rose will be the more common symbol of this order in the New Age. The complete mysteries of these symbols can only be revealed through the esoteric path of initiation, which I offer through the graded teachings of my organization, the Mystic Light Society. However, I will reveal that to even wear these symbols in any form, especially if it is carved in crystal, will bring a vibration of universal harmony to the person who wears it.

The story of Christian Rosenkreuze is a very interesting one and I would like to share it with you at this time, so as to prepare a foundation of understanding which will introduce the reader to the Masters of Wisdom. Christian Rosenkreuze, also known by the initials C.R.C. (Christian Rose Cross) was aware of his inclination to secret knowledge at a young age. He was of German origin and descended of noble parents. He was placed in a convent at the age of five to receive his education, and learned Latin and Greek. He met a certain man known as Brother P.A.L. who became his mentor, and at the age of fifteen accompanied this brother on a journey to the Holy Land. The brother became ill and died in Cypress but young Christian continued the journey. He never made it to the Holy Land because while in Arabia he heard of a group of advanced mystics who lived in a city called Damcar. He had this inner desire to find this illuminated society and upon doing so was welcomed by them as though they had been expecting him.

The Magi initiated the young man into the mysteries of the universe and the Arabic Tongue. He was allowed to read a sacred magical book known as "M", and this he translated from Arabic to Latin. After a total of three years of mystic studies with this group he went to Egypt and studied two more years with an illustrious group of masters, who initiated him further and imparted the knowledge of herbs, and how to communicate with the beings of the four elements. After this period of five years young Christian Rosenkreuze travelled to Spain to share his knowledge with the learned philosophers who gathered in that country. However, the advanced wisdom which he now possessed was too much for the advanced thinkers of that part of the world, and he received little recognition. So, the young man returned to his native Germany, built a secluded house in the forest and spent five years reducing his powerful mystic knowledge to a graded system of instruction. After this his house became known as "the House of the Holy Spirit" for he invited the sick of mind and body to come for spiritual healing and instruction. During this time he chose three advanced people and initiated them into his system of mystical philosophy, thus the Fraternity of the Rosy Cross began.

The knowledge which Christian Rosenkreuze discovered and taught was not new for there is evidence that such knowledge existed in ancient Atlantis and Egypt. Even Jesus the Christ taught a secret wisdom to his inner circle of disciples. As for the mysterious masters who welcomed this man as though they expected him, I can believe such an account based on my own experience. When I was still a child I began to meet people who seemed to know exactly what I was thinking and gave me bits of information and instructions regarding my own path. Several of these people became friends of my parents and when they would visit they would answer my questions in an uncanny manner as soon as I was alone with them. This was so unusual because my parents were not into this type of knowledge and therefore I could not speak to them of what was on my mind. This experience which repeated itself again and again was special because perfect strangers were able to know exactly what was in my heart and gave me the necessary instruction to further my development on the path of light. Such people, fraternities and societies as we have considered are inspired and guided by a higher power-spirits of an advanced evolution known by such terms as Ascended Masters, the Great White Brotherhood, Masters of the Wisdom, and by many other terms. Now it is time for the reader to become familiar with the Masters and how they can help us at this time.

MASTERS OF WISDOM:

Humanity is constantly evolving into higher states of awareness and advancement. However, there have always been individuals who have made greater advancement at a faster pace because of their sincere effort towards self realization, beyond the average. Such persons have transcended much of their Karma and the limitations of human existence. These people have become masters, and therefore when they pass out of physical existence, they become

what is known as an Ascended Master, or one who has ascended
beyond the need to incarnate in physical life again and has transcended the limitations of human existence. The purpose of these
illustrious beings of light is to guide those of us who walk the
path of regeneration so that we may become like them. They are
the real power behind all secret mystical societies and efforts
towards true self realization. Although there are many such beings,
we will acquaint the reader with a few of them now.

JESUS THE CHRIST:

Jesus the Christ was a self realized Son of God who fully manifested the Cosmic Christ. Although the misguided religious leaders of recent centuries have misinterpreted his true message, there has always been secret groups such as the Rosy Cross who have preserved the inner teachings of Jesus. Our Mystic Light Society is one of the modern day institutions which offer the secret teachings of Jesus and the nine initiations of the mysteries in a graded instruction format.

This great soul transcended all dimensions and returned to this level willingly so that he might perfect the existing mystical systems and show us a more perfect way. Thus his mission was, indeed, the sacrifice of the ages. His true message concerning the crucifixion, the cleansing blood and other misinterpreted doctrines is part of a secret teaching which can only be given as one progresses on the path of initiation. Since these things cannot be written in a book for the general public, the reader is invited to write the author for information regarding the Inner Teachings of Christ.

The Biblical book of Hebrews reveals some hints to the arcane nature of Jesus' mission. It tells of how he learned his early lessons through suffering and self deniel so that he could return to become the Saviour. It is known among initiates that the beloved master is now the head of the Great White Brotherhood and serves as world teacher to bring humanity to an awareness which will increase as we advance in the New Age. His other mystic names are "Esu" and "Sananda". Anyone who utters any of his names with devotion will receive an instant blessing from him.

COUNT ST.GERMAIN:
St. Germain lived in eighteenth century France and was

acclaimed as an adept in the art of Alchemy, and the man who never grows old. Several aging contemporaries saw him and recorded

that although many years had passed, he still appeared to be about forty years of age. Several witnesses even saw him years after his supposed death. St. Germain still lives in an immortalized body (a body which has been transformed into an etherial substance by a spiritual technique of raising the rate of vibration), and is a member of the Great White Brotherhood. He serves as administrator of the Holy Spirit through the Violet Flame Energy.

Count St. Germain feigned death during the time of the French Revolution that he might emerge as a different character in the new world. He had a dream to unite the countries of Europe, but failed because of lack of cooperation. Here in the new world he succeeded. He worked closely with two initiated mystics who were Benjamin Franklin and George Washington, and with their help he inspired the founding of the United States of America. However, he has appeared from time to time as the Count St. Germain for the purpose of helping to establish mystical organizations destined to publish the truth of the ages.

On page 41 the illustration of St. Germain reveals one of the Rosicrucian symbols: a cross with a lily and a rose. He has requested that I impart the following information concerning this symbol. The lily is symbolic of the "Lily of the Valley" spoken of in the Bible. The plant known as the Lily of the Valley grows in the shade and is pure white and very fragrant. This means that we must realize that although we may be in the dark (shade) about certain things, if we keep a pure line of thinking in harmony with the divine truth as we know it, we will be filled with the White Light of Christ, and ascend into full bloom as the "Rose of Sharon". The mystical term "sub Rosa" means "under the Rose"; this means to keep the secrets which we have learned in times of dark experiences (lily of the valley) when we have blossomed as the rose. The Rose of Sharon is symbolic of when we raise our consciousness into the heart or place of regeneration and compassion. The cross tells us that we can raise our consciousness in this physical life even though we may have seeming limitations on the cross of physical matter, or the world of the four elements. Thus you have the meaning of this symbol for your consideration and meditation. This is why the new age version of this symbol will be a heart and a rose.

KUTHUMI:

Koot Hoomi Lal Singh (also known as Master K.H. and Kuthumi), shares with Jesus the office of world teacher. He lived here during the last century and helped to found the science of modern Psychology. His incarnations have been impressive, including Pythagoras, Balthazar (one of the three wisemen), St. Francis of Assisi and others.

He lives in an etheric temple of illumination where he forms an etheric image of every disciple of the path. By this method he is able to follow the progress of the disciple.

EL MORYA:

This great being is the Master of Synthesis who inspires the blending of belief systems and philosophies into one unit of truth manifested. It is the desire of El Morya that all true disciples of the path find the strand of truth which unites all religions.

His past incarnations include that of King Arthur, Thomas a' Becket and Sir Thomas More. He heads the Darjeeling Council of the Great White Brotherhood. He administers discipline through experience to advanced souls preparing for higher initiation.

KUAN YIN:

This illustrious Lady Ascended Master is the Oriental representative of the Mother God aspect, as Mother Mary is to the Occidental world. However, as we enter the New Age, more people in the west are becoming aware of Kuan Yin (pronounced Kwan - a like ah- Yin -like tin). She is known as the Goddess of mercy for she prays for disciples of the path, that they have the opportunity to work out karma by service in the work of light. She is ever there, as a loving mother, to assist all who invoke her.

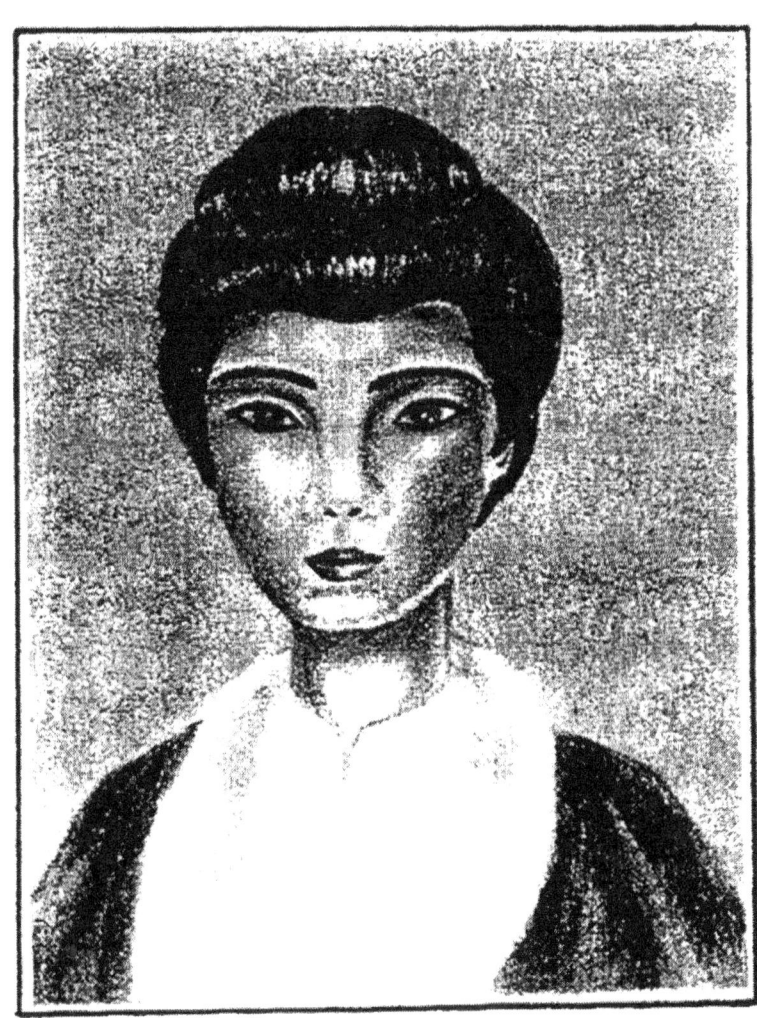

MASTER JOHN:

This glorious master is the entity that manifested as the young Apostle John, the beloved. Master John was the author of the original Gospel of St. John and the Book of Revelations. He has truly blended with his "I AM Presence" but still projects a fragment of his oversoul here in this physical dimension through a living mystic adept, of whom little can be said here. This is because it was the will of his master Jesus that a part of him remain here to guide humanity until the end of the age. From the place of Light he channels his vital messages as Master John. It is he who inspired the author to write books and found the Mystic Light Society.

HOW TO CONTACT THE MASTERS OF WISDOM:

There are several methods to contact and receive help from the Masters, and I will reveal a few now. However, as stated earlier, some methods should only be revealed through initiation in a graded system of mystical instruction; the reader is invited to write the author for further information regarding the Inner Teachings of Christ.

THE IMPORTANT FACTOR IN SUCCESSFUL CONTACT:

To successfully invoke the help of the Masters we must first make sure that our intentions are pure. By that I mean that we should never seek their help in accomplishing selfish or evil goals, such as controlling others for personal gain or lust, unlawful monetary gain, or any other negative thing. If we attempt to secure their help in negative matters we will only find a closed door, and will have to go through severe discipline. Therefore, make sure you have pure intentions. Then we must be on the path of light by active study of metaphysical principles. If we do the best we can we can rest assured that we will attract the attention of a master of wisdom. At times they may contact you before you have the chance to invoke them. This may transpire in one or more different ways, such as through dreams, visions or omens. You may even meet a mysterious person who will give you a vital message.

THE BEST TIME TO MAKE CONTACT:

Any time that you can meditate and pray quietly is a good time. However, the special night of the Great White Lodge is on Thursday Night from 9:P.M. to 12 Midnight. You can go according to your own time zone. It is best to sit quietly in a room with just a candle burning.

THE GREAT INVOCATION:

Here is the special prayer which places you in contact with the purpose and power of the Masters of Wisdom. Meditate upon the words as you speak them with heartfelt sincere devotion. Say this prayer as much as possible in addition to just Thursday night, for the Masters have given us this prayer to link us to their Guidance.

"FROM THE POINT OF LIGHT WITHIN THE MIND OF GOD
   LET LIGHT STREAM FORTH INTO THE MINDS OF MEN.
     LET LIGHT DESCEND ON EARTH.

FROM THE POINT OF LOVE WITHIN THE HEART OF GOD
   LET LOVE STREAM FORTH INTO THE HEARTS OF MEN.
     MAY CHRIST RETURN TO EARTH.

FROM THE CENTRE WHERE THE WILL OF GOD IS KNOWN
   LET PURPOSE GUIDE THE LITTLE WILLS OF MEN -
     THE PURPOSE WHICH THE MASTERS KNOW AND SERVE.

FROM THE CENTRE WHICH WE CALL THE RACE OF MEN
   LET THE PLAN OF LOVE AND LIGHT WORK OUT
     AND MAY IT SEAL THE DOOR WHERE EVIL DWELLS

LET LIGHT AND LOVE AND POWER RESTORE THE PLAN ON EARTH.

And these are the words of power by which you may invoke the power of the Christ and the Masters of Wisdom to help and guide you in your daily life. Pray this prayer often and you will feel a great change taking place within you. Do not reveal this to just anyone, but only people who are aware of the New Age and on the path as you are.

SECRET SIGNS OF CONTACT:

Before repeating the Great Invocation you should place your hands in the original praying hands position as this will help you greatly. You are to arrange your hands in the following manner:

1. Place the tips of your thumbs together;

2. Place the tips of all your other fingers together;

3. Place your hands with thumbs touching the Solar Plexus area (your stomach, just below the rib cage).

   You should be able to look down at your hands and notice a triangle or pyramid formation.

THE PROTECTION SIGN:

When you feel that your mind is being attacked by negative thoughts or evil forces touch the tip of your left thumb to the base of your little finger, then bend all of your fingers downward over the thumb so as cover the thumb in your palm. you can do this anytime and anyplace when you feel the need to do so.

PART 2-THE MYSTIC LIGHT COMMUNICATIONS

The following material is of great importance and inspiration. They are channelled messages from the Ascended Masters of wisdom. The purpose of these communications is to educate the student of the path concerning the Great White Brotherhood and the universal wisdom of Spirit. May you receive them in the same spirit in which they are shared-the spirit of divine love.

Communication #1.
MASTER K.H. (KUTHUMI) SPEAKS ON THE PURPOSE AND POSITION OF THE HIERARCHY:

Hail, brothers and sisters on the Path of God's Light. In this transmission I would like to make clear the position and purpose of the Hierarchy.

In all ages there has been a body of spiritual masters who have escaped the bonds of human limitation by sacrifice of the lower self, dedication to God and service to others. These blessed souls evolve in an emotional, moral, mental and spiritual sense until they become masters of the Divine Wisdom. They carefully observe the experience of all nations at every epoch, and preserve the knowledge gained through this experience. During times of global darkness the Hierarchy inspires humankind to search for and apply the Divine Truth of the Ages. They do this through world leaders, philosophers and metaphysical teachers. The ancient wisdom teaching is ever in our care and we work with special individuals who have proven themselves worthy of true knowledge: These we instruct and initiate into the highest form of Psychic development that they may become the channels and instruments through which the ancient teachings are rediscovered and brought to light. Those whom we instruct can become like us if they continue on the path of unselfish service.

We have been known by several names of which I will recall to clear up any misconception arising from them. The first I will explain is that of the "Great White Brotherhood". Some have deduced that the word "white" implies the white race. This is an error as the Hierarchy is composed of great souls who have

evolved from all races and nations. The word implies that we are of the White Light of the Christ, in opposition to the hierarchy of darkness. The word "Brotherhood" should also come under our clarification: Until recently women have been considered inferior to men in society. However, there are also many women within the Hierarchy. In God's sight there is no separation between male and female for we are one in the spiritual domain. Therefore, the term brotherhood was allowed at a time when society's awareness was limited in respect to gender. Furthermore, as the term "mankind" includes the entire human race, both male and female, so does the term "brotherhood". We have been called the Magi or Kings of the East. This name is sympathetic to us because we have truly mastered the sacred magical forces of nature, and as the Sun rises in the East, so have we arisen in the Inner Light. We have been called the true and hidden Rosicrucian Order and this is so, for when any mystery school uses that term in its true sense they refer to us, the inner adepts and masters who inspire their activity. Furthermore, we initiate the faithful student in the mystery of the Rosy Cross which is the beginning of their ascension into freedom. In the early days of the Theosophical Society we were called Mahatmas. This name is also in harmony with our order for it means Great (Maha) Soul (Atma). The most recent names given to our order are "the Hierarchy" and "Masters of the Wisdom". Beloved students, I have said these things that you may realize the oneness of the people of God which transcends the limitations of terminology. We may now continue with further consideration of our purpose.

God desires to bring about a greater manifestation of the Hierarchy to seekers of light for the purpose of correcting religious and metaphysical error which has prevailed in recent times. In the past we have been misquoted by some of the channels who have adulterated our message with their own incorrect ideas. The wisdom which we transmit is a medicine of sound doctrine which cures all ills at every level of human existence if it is received and given completely. Our teaching is not devoid of religious conviction as some have taught. However, we teach religion as a science, instructing students in the techniques and systems which liberate them from illusion so that they may discover the great revelation within and understand life's mysteries.

Such understanding brings a great power into manifestation within the knower's life. The development of this power comes not with the reading of many books, nor with moving about from teaching to teaching. This power is given to the faithful disciple of Christ who follows a true scientific path. This power is witheld from the doubtful and selfish. But to those who believe and serve, the power shall be given. Therefore, the student must purge himself from all undesirable motives and seek to attain so that he may serve God and his fellows better. How quickly one attains this development depends on their faith, dedication and willingness to work within the grades of light.

Do not seek this power of which I speak for the purpose of gaining riches to satisfy egotistical pride. Rather, seek to find harmony within yourself and good things will come to you with less effort. Did not our beloved Jesus teach this?

I wish to make clear that, while some metaphysical teachers have tried to lessen the importance of Jesus' mission, we fully acknowledge his office as world saviour and channel of Christ's love to the world. He is the head of the Hierarchy and the chief corner stone of the mystical church. Organized religion has, for the most part, made mockery of the true mission and purpose of

Jesus the Christ. Therefore, some who find a portion of metaphysical truth assume that Jesus is just a product of organized religion. The truth is that Jesus was a human who, in past times, climbed the ladder of progression and ascended back to God. The apostolic writer of the Book of Hebrews reveals much concerning the ascension of Jesus from humanity to divinity. After his perfection he chose out of love for a humanity in darkness, to return to the lower world that he might provide a pure temple through which the Christ aspect of God could assist humankind. Beware of teachers who promise to enlighten you without any religious faith. It is true that organized religion does not teach the complete wisdom. However, divine truth is hidden within its scriptures: the Holy Bible, Bhagavad-Gita, the Koran and other sacred writings are records of an ancient wisdom religion, revealed in parables according to the understanding of the cultures to whom they were revealed. The initiated disciple may discover and understand the true message of all Holy Scriptures.

At this time the Christ sits at the right hand of Sanat Kumara (the name of the planetary manifestation of God) in the celestial Shamballa, also called the Kingdom of God. This place of light is the Third Heaven from which the Love of God flows to the Human Race. Sanat Kumara is the Lord over Planet Earth. He is also called the Ancient of Days and is the greatest expression of the Heavenly Father which man is able to grasp at the present stage of development.

As Christ was about to withdraw from the physical world he promised his disciples that he would send another comforter, the Spirit of Truth or the Holy Spirit. The present administrator of the Holy Spirit is the Master Rakoczi, also known to students

of the path as St. Germain. This illustrious master now sits on the left hand of Sanat Kumara, and is he who kindles the fire of true devotion within the hearts of all sincere disciples regardless of their path or teacher. St. Germain is also the maker of nations, for he has always inspired men of truth to perpetuate the way of freedom and justice. He is working with Master Jesus to bring about a revival of spiritual interest within the human consciousness for the purpose of ushering in the Aquarian Age. St. Germain is the Master of the Violet Ray of Supreme Spiritual Unfoldment and instructs disciples in the art of transmutation, by which the fire of the human soul is transmuted into the Violet Flame of the Holy Spirit.

I, Kuthumi, hold the office of World Teacher with Master Jesus. My work is with disciples about to enter the path of initiation. When any young person begins to come of age I will contact them through subtle thoughts which suggest that they seek the true path of life. In the event that an advanced disciple or adept reincarnates I will manifest myself to them at some point in their lives. Such was the case of my channel William: Saint Germain, Master Morya and I appeared to him at a crucial time when he needed our help in revealing what was to be his future work for, and later within the Hierarchy.

In my retreat I form an ethereal image of every person who enters the path. Through this image I may observe the progress, success and failures of all true disciples. When a disciple allows the illusions of life to hold sway through negative thoughts, slothfulness or greed in any form, there falls a mist over the image which dims the light of the soul. Although I know these things, I will not interfere unless the student asks for my help. If the disciple continues to falter I may withdraw myself for a

season and leave the prodigal to go his own way until he realizes, through the lessons of suffering, that the way of rebellion is a path of many tears and snares. I bid you peace, love and light.
I AM KUTHUMI.

Communication #2.
MASTER EL MORYA SPEAKS ON ONENESS:

Greetings, dear ones. In this communication I will teach further on the Hierarchy as already started by our beloved Kuthumi.

All blend into one: all human races are one, all religions are one, all philosophies are one. When light passes through a prism it manifests as seven colors, but is only one light in seven expressions. The true religion is truth itself which is found within the sanctuary of wisdom, and this sanctuary is within the heart. When the disciple reads sacred books he partakes of divine knowledge but only at the objective level. When the disciple meditates upon what he has read and reviews it until he realizes it, it then becomes a living wisdom-divine knowledge becomes the disciple and the disciple becomes it.

All religions contain a portion of truth but inner wisdom is the whole truth. This inner wisdom may not be known in its fullness by every student, but it is an unfolding wisdom which becomes more visible and expanded as the student is able to understand it. This takes effort and patience. Religions are like the color vibrations of the prism-truth is the light which impregnates the prism.

Each student who enters the path of true occultism is noticed by the Hierarchy, but only in a casual sense. The student who perseveres in his quest gains the attention of a Master of Wisdom and will be contacted by the master, either directly or through the student's teacher at the appointed time. Many are those who approach the Temple of Wisdom, some enter its outer court; few are those who enter the Sanctum Sanctorum. Most students are too busy trying to rob the attention of the teacher from their fellows as though this will evolve them any faster. Or they may foolishly think, after a brief training, that they themselves are qualified to teach-they may even seek to teach the teacher. The student who wishes to represent the Hierarchy must first be tried, permitted to pass through the initiations before they see the master.

Some people hold fast to the illusion that they are important enough to demand the personal instruction of a master, or an abundance of attention from their individual instructor or guru when, in reality, they have not yet proved themselves worthy of such attention. When such attention is given to a neophyte it is a favor. If they would see the master often they must master their lower ego which is the personalized devil of unregenerated man. It is this devil which causes students to rummage through the points of occult teaching, praising the doctrines which suit their fancy and frowning upon the points which reveal their ignorance. It is this devil which causes students to turn away from the true teacher who may uncover their illusions with the sometime indignant word of the two-edged sword, and seek out a teacher who tickles their ears with flattery. It is this devil which causes the student to escape the responsibility of the path by finding fault with the teacher. Therefore, realize that if you have been directed to a teacher it is he or she who is your living access to the Masters of Wisdom, if indeed they be a

representative of the Hierarchy. When you have found your teacher you must humble yourself to receive all that you can. You may reach a stage of development so that you may become a teacher of your own students, but while in the presence of your guru you are the student. Such humility gains the attention of the Elders. If you can not endure the tests of an unascended master of wisdom (your teacher) how can you survive the evaluation of the Hierarchy.

We do not force anyone to enter or remain on the path. That is a personal decision that each student must make. In the same way, we do not make accomodations to hold a student. We will always help if we are requested to do so, and if it would not interfere with the karmic progress of the student. The student must work to maintain thoughts of love, beauty and truth. This will create a link between the student and the Hierarchy. By making a constant effort to think, feel and speak in the light a student may rid himself of destructive thoughts and emotions.
I AM EL MORYA

Communication #3.
MASTER JESUS, THE CHRIST SPEAKS ON REASONS AND EXCUSES:

My dearly beloved. I will call your attention to the word "awareness". I ask you a question: Where is your awareness, and to what level of vibration is your attention directed?

Are you only aware of the physical things for their own sake or is your attention on the physical things with the intention of transforming them into tools for spiritual advancement?

I say to you that your attention should be directed within and without. Within to discover who you are and without only to bless and transform the outer things.

When I spoke to the multitudes during my earthlife, my teaching was given in shadows and illustrations. But to the special ones who followed me with all their heart, I taught the inner meaning of all things. To my faithful who were with me in the house I opened the book of all wisdom freely. To be in the house means to direct your attention within: are you not the house of the Holy Spirit, the Temple of the Lord? Go within by meditation and prayer that you may learn from the Inner Master.

People who fail are the ones who give reasons and excuses for not knowing themselves and mastering their outer and inner world.

When one really wishes to do something there is no reason or excuse to prevent it. Therefore, cultivate a desire to know yourself and realize that this is the only path to liberation. If you persevere with your contemplation of the cosmic you will begin to take an interest in all spiritual matters and grow from them.

I spoke a parable that it is not wise to sew a piece of new cloth to an old garment as the tear would be made worse. It is also unwise to pour new wine into old skins.

The meaning of this is that you cannot contain the increased energy of spirit in pure form when your life is beset by negativity and personal conflicts. Therefore, strive to be at peace, so that

your temple is prepared for the higher vibration of spirit.
I AM JESUS.

Communication #4.
MASTER ST. GERMAIN SPEAKS ON SADNESS:

There are times when sadness comes to one for no apparent reason. You can search your heart and mind and find no answer for the emptiness you feel. It is at just such a time that you are missing your Divine Father. When I was in your physical world, I often felt a longing that could not be filled by anything or anyone I could see around me.

I was an intelligent man, very active with possessions and power, yet I felt alone. People around me loved me but could not touch me.

I share this with you because if you experience what I speak of, it is best to flow with it and know God loves you and is calling you. Find a place to be alone and let your mind empty. Say, "here I am, Lord" and feel the presence of the Everlasting God with you. A soul that goes through this is usually very advanced and pure.
I AM ST. GERMAIN.

Communication #5.
THE SPIRIT OF TRUTH (THE HOLY SPIRIT) SPEAKS TO SEEKERS:

Dear precious ones, chosen of the New Age, hear the words of life which I speak to you now: You are chosen because you are a seeker of divine truth, untouched by human dogmas which taint the truth of God. You have been directed to this path because you have asked for help. Your call has been answered.

The legions of darkness have doubled their efforts in attempting to cast doubt in the minds of true believers. Beware of the way in which they influence you without your knowledge. These forces of darkness cause one to find fault with their teacher, become indifferent to the teaching, become slothful in their spiritual work, and above all other things they cause the disciple to doubt his own progress. Although the legions of darkness are busy at work, there is another force at work with which they must deal.

The legions of light are also busy trying to awaken the sleeping spirits of men to the great new day of God's manifestation in the world. You are among the Legions of Light if you do not turn your back on the truth. Now is the time for reaping the harvest, for the Great Day of the Lord is at hand.
I AM THE SPIRIT OF TRUTH.

Communication #6.
ASHTAR, COMMANDER-IN-CHIEF OF THE SPACE FEDERATION SPEAKS ON BALANCE OF THE 1980's IN DESTINY:

Greetings my earthly brothers and sisters. In the three-fold power of the Cosmic Unity I come to you in the essence of the One Light. The early part of 1985 was a time of great battle between the forces of light and darkness. The numerical symbolism of 1985 is significant when it is mathematically reduced to a single digit vibration; if you add these numbers you will have 23. Add

these and you have number 5. This is the number of the pyramid for it is composed of four corners at the base and the point at the apex. Man is created with a built-in reminder of this Cosmic Revelation, for man has five extremities which are two arms, two legs, and a head. Therefore, 1985 has been a year of rebuilding the states of consciousness within each individual. Terrorism, famine and local violence has beset those of a lower vibration. On the other hand, those who are tuned into the light have initiated new acts of love and peace to fellow humans.

The single digit vibration of 1986 is 6. Therefore, 1986 will be a year of further progress for the Great White Brotherhood and the Space Federation in behalf of humanity on earth. Many strange signs and wonders will be perceived in the cycles of nature. There will be more outbursts in both the nature of men and from within planet earth. Yet, in the midst of all undesirable events, there will be a great awakening in the minds of the elect. Remember the Biblical example of how the Christ turned water into wine from six pots of water; and how the creation took place in six days. Therefore, be encouraged and know that during 1986 you will be transformed into a greater expression of the chosen of God if you remain strong.

The year 1987 will vibrate to the number 7. This is the Sacred Number of Perfection. Therefore, you will see a great spiritual awakening during that year. This great awakening will be initiated by the combined efforts of the Space Federation and the Masters of the Wisdom through our earth channels. Such channels will find themselves suddenly locked into the seventh octave of the Violet Ray, and be able to control events in the Fourth Dimensional field of manifestation. This will result in new awareness among the general inhabitants of earth and many

will begin to search out the illuminated channels.

Looking further ahead 1988 will vibrate to the number 8, and this signifies the point beyond perfection. During this year, many will take the extra steps to work more than ever in cooperation with the Hierarchy of Light. Some will vanish from earth because they would have proven themselves worthy and able to assist us aboard our vehicles.

The year 1989 will vibrate to the number 9, and this is the number of initiation. Some will take the mark of the beast, which is the vibration of 9 in the ultra-red scale of diabolical manifestation. Others will take the mark of the chosen of Christ, which is the vibration of 9 in the ultra-violet scale of Godly manifestation.

1990 is the year of number 10. That year, with its remaining decade, will see many events of major significance. The nature of these events will seal the doom of forces which hinder the progress of God and the day of divine intervention will be at hand. The children of perdition will run in utter madness to escape the intense vibrations of the Light. But the children of God will become stronger and more assertive as a ruling force in the New Age.

My precious brothers and sisters, know that we have intervened and have saved humankind from its self-imposed destruction many times. Even as you read these words, there are five tons of explosive weapons to every human on planet earth; famine creeps over the planet like a cloud of darkness as 48 million people die of starvation every year; Criminal and political terrorism is spreading around the globe like a cancer; the economy is in

serious trouble worldwide, and men's hearts are more afraid than ever before. Yet, many have forgotten that they are indeed their brother's keeper. Do not be overcome by the madness of the hour: Look toward the Light of God and be protected. I now give you a plan which you can be a part of. Study the messages now available to you through this channel and pray often as you behold the rising Sun. Think of the words, RA-MA-SEH as you greet the sunrise. I will speak to you again. Be at peace.
I AM ASHTAR.

Communication #7.
MASTER KUAN YIN SPEAKS ON DIVINE MOTHER:

Dearly beloved, both the male and female aspects are required to create a new human life. Even so, the Father Aspect of God is incomplete without the Divine Mother Aspect.

Father God impregnates the material universe with his life and intelligence, but the material universe is the Mother God manifestation which receives the seed of life and germinates it to come forth as intelligent life. Therefore look upon the matter around you as Mother God and you will tune in to its higher manifestation. Attune the material part of your being to the higher vibration of the Christ and you will become the spiritual bride of Christ.
I AM KUAN YIN

Communication #8.
MASTER JOHN SPEAKS ON THE BEAST:

My fellow Light Workers, I greet you in the power of the

Christ. In this communication I warn you of the power of the Beast that I wrote about in the Book of Revelation. Already, the power of anti-christ has taken over the minds of the rebellious ones who have mentally sold out to Satan and have turned their backs on the true way. Many religious people even feed the Beast and do not realize it because their minds have been darkened to the higher concepts of truth, love, peace and mercy.

At this time there is an increased assault upon the minds of the righteous for the purpose of leading them away from their true purpose. You may feel this assault in strange feelings as though some strange thing has happened to you. Do not be alarmed when this happens. Just keep your heart pure and your thoughts of a high order of thinking.

Face the sunrise as much as possible and think, "the Sun of Righteousness is arising with healing in his wings". As you meditate on these words realize that the Christ does arise, as the sun, to bring healing and refreshment to you when you seek for the Christ within. Also, meditate upon the ancient Egyptian Symbol below, as often as you can. Gaze upon it when you need help and encouragement, for it is symbolic of the Christ arising to give light on your path. It also means that by your sincere efforts you will raise the consciousness of your own being.
Peace be with you always.
I AM JOHN

PENTAGRAMAGICK™

William Alexander Oribello

PENTAGRAMAGICK™

BY
William Alexander Oribello

First edition privately published
Copyright 1989-All rights reserved.

Second edition published 1992
Copyright 1992-All rights reserved

The information in this booklet is based on the research and experience of the author. No Supernatural, medical or other effects can be guaranteed. The practitioner is responsible for the practice of these techniques, according to their belief.

Always use wisdom and common sense in working with the potent magick described in this booklet. Keep your personal work confidential. Remember the Magickal Command: To know -To will -To dare -To keep silent.

Blessed Be!

INTRODUCTION

For thousands of years, the Pentagram has been a superior symbol of Divine Truth and for the Sacred Magickal Art. Such great philosophers as Leanardo DaVince and Pythagoras have used this symbol to illustrate the hidden mysteries of life, (as in DaVinci's illustration of the "Microcosmic Man").

The Pentagram may be interpreted at several levels of magickal and spiritual philosophy. At one level it can represent the Five Wounds of Christ; on the head, (caused by the crown of thorns), the two hands and two feet. At another level it is symbolic of the Five Elements of Magickal Philosophy; the point at the top represents the element of Ether/Spirit, the lower left hand point is symbolic of the element of Earth, the lower right hand point is symbolic of the element of Fire, the upper left hand point is symbolic of the element of Air, the upper right hand point is symbolic of the element of Water. Although the Pentagram is predominantly a symbol of Earth, we can see that it also contains the other elements with it, as exemplified by the traditional attributions of the five points to the five elements, as already explained.

According to occult teachings, when the Pentagram appears with a single point uppermost it represents positive magick; and when it appears with two points uppermost it represent negative magick.

Although it is a common belief that the two point uppermost Pentagram is an evil symbol, in the advanced mysteries it means this:

The Inverted Pentagram is symbolic of the human who is not fully developed in higher consciousness but is still walking the path of lessons in the world of the four elements. The Pentagram with one point upwards is symbolic of one who rules over the world of the four elements.

The mass media and organized religion has been responsible for much of the wrong information in reference to the Pentagram. For example, they may focus on a case where a sadistic killer who has a background of occult studies, and who may use the symbol of the Pentagram in connection with his/her crimes. He/she may even, upon being caught, say that this symbol influenced him/her to commit the crimes. So a misinformed media jumps on the bandwagon, lumping all occult teachings together (including their symbols) as being evil. But what they seem to ignore is the fact that there have also been many sadistic crimes committed by people who claim that Jesus or Almighty God made them do it. Yet they do not persecute organized religion. I say this: Persecute anyone who breaks the law and harms others. But do not prosecute a certain religion or philosophy just because the criminal says he/she was connected with it at some point in life. It is narrow minded and ignorant to condemn the occult, just because someone who studied occult teachings turned out to be a criminal, just as it would also be narrow minded and ignorant to condemn traditional religion when one who studied it turns out to be a criminal.

So, why do some people try so hard to convince you that the Pentagram is an evil symbol? The answer to that, my friend, is simply this: Some of the organized religious organizations, who are still trying to keep humanity in the dark ages, have become desperate. Their reason is that so many people are getting tired of receiving no real answers to their vital questions. Many are leaving organized religion, and finding the answers in the many avenues of new age/metaphysical studies. But friend, this is a day of new enlightenment, when that which was hidden for ages will be shouted from the rooftops.

In ages past, the mystic Magi used the awesome power of the Pentagram, and it was the intuitive power derived from this symbol that guided members of this group to the newborn child, who was destined to refine the existing systems of magick into a glorious blending of power techniques that could be used by anyone. At the same time and before, great numbers of people, all over the world, celebrated what came to be known as "The Old Religion", with all of its magickal secrets for real success, health and happiness. This old religion, also known as "Wicca", (meaning "the Craft of the Wise), used the awesome power of the Pentagram in its sacred magickal rites.

But the new religion, formed many hundreds of years ago, in the name of Jesus, condemned the old religion as being evil. Every new religion turns the gods of the old religion into the devils of the new religion. Any thinking person will realize that the new religion has brought nothing but choas into the world, just look around you.

The truth of the matter is that many of the Biblical characters, including Moses, Solomon, and Jesus practiced the Craft of the Wise. The British Museum has many manuscripts of magickal practice, such as "The Sixth and Seventh Books of Moses", "The Lesser and Greater Keys of Solomon". Both of these works have been published in different nations, and both contain magickal talismans using the Pentagram. In addition to this, the recently translated "Nag Hamadi Library", shed new light on the fact that Jesus' original teachings were far different from the accepted teachings of modern Christianity. There are also several Magickal Grimoires, written by Christian Mystics during the middle ages, which employ the power of the Pentagram.

Here is the bottom line- this is a sacred magickal symbol that can and will make you a powerful person in every way, if you will but use it properly. Turn your back on fear, hesitation and ignorance and turn toward the Light of Understanding and Power. Claim your right to greater health, happiness and prosperity by using the Pentagram, beginning right now.

1. THE FIVE FOLD POWER OF THE PENTAGRAM

Each of the five points of the Pentagram is attributed to one of the five elements of magickal lore. Below is a list of these, along with their legendary powers.

1. Ether (Spirit), also termed "Askasha", holds the power to assist us in matters of spiritual development, higher consciousness, etc., and its Magickal Gate is the top point of the Pentagram.

2. Earth holds the power to assist us in all material matters, such as money, business, personal relationships, etc., and it Magickal Gate is the lower left hand point of the Pentagram.

3. Fire holds the power to assist us in matters of the heart and emotions, such as loving relationships, passionate love, rivalry, overcoming enemies, etc., and its Magickal Gate is the lower right hand point of the Pentagram.

4. Air holds the power to assist us in matters of mind such as studies, exams, philosophy, thought, etc., and its Magickal Gate is the upper left hand point of the Pentagram.

5. Water holds the power to assist us in matters of healing, peace of mind, the harmonious blending of thought and emotion, the realm of departed souls, etc., and its Magickal Gate is the upper right hand point of the Pentagram.

The five points of the Pentagram are five Magickal Gates, through which we can tap into the cosmic resources of the Universal Mind to attract the right situations into our lives. See figure #1, below.

FIGURE #1.

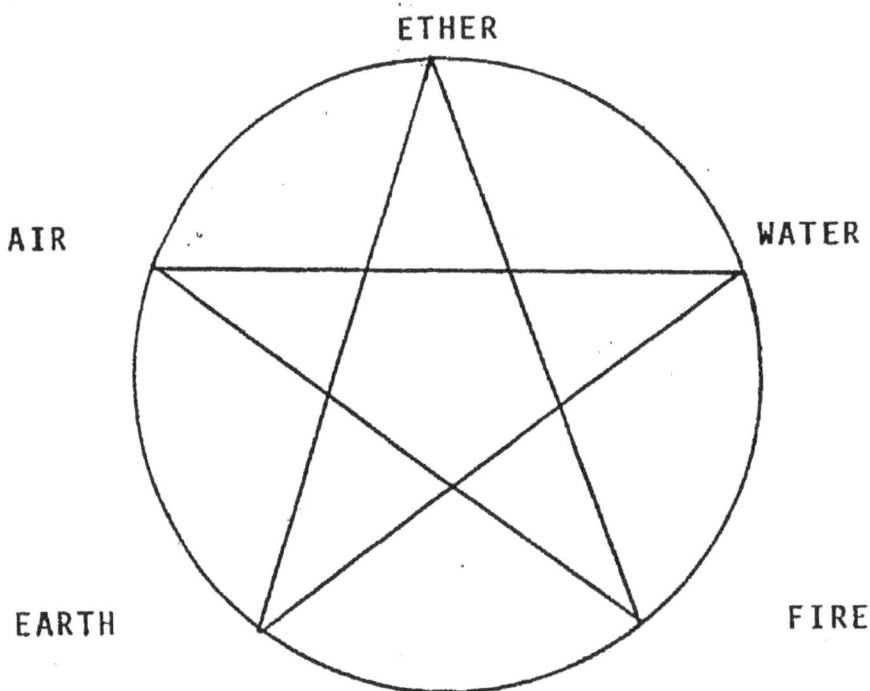

At the end of your book, on the back cover, is a large illustration of the Pentagram. You may take this to any quick-print or copy shop to have copies made, so that you can perform the magickal experiments that I will teach you.

You will notice that I illustrate the Pentagram within a circle. The circle is symbolic of the Universal Mind or Supreme Being (God & Goddess) in total power. It is also symbolic of the Protection Circle and the Magickal Circle that encompasses

the practitioner of this Sacred Craft.

I will teach you how to use the five Magickal Gates of the Pentagram, for every human need. This method of using the Pentagram has never been revealed before. You can make several copies of the large Pentagram from the back cover of this booklet. Color it according to my instructions, using a crayon or felt-tip marker. You can have the large Pentagram copied on plain white paper or card stock, or on fancy parchment type paper, depending on what the copy shop has available. You will also need certain herbs to perform the experiments.

2. USING THE PENTAGRAM FOR MATERIAL NEEDS

When you wish to apply the Power of the Pentagram in matters of money, business, gambling, and earthy personal relationships, do the following things. Take a copy of the large Pentagram (from now on, I will refer to copies of the Pentagram as "Pentagramagick Energizers") and color it green.

In Figure #1 you will notice that the lower left hand point of the Pentagram is the Magickal Gate of Earth, for material matters. Place your Pentagramagick Energizer on a table, making sure that the lower left hand point of the large Pentagram is pointing to the North.

Write down your request in a few words on a small sheet of paper, and place it (with writing visible) on the center of the Pentgramagick Energizer. Place a small amount of Vervain within the lower left hand point. Stand over the table gazing at the Pentagram, facing the direction revealed in Figure #2.

FIGURE #2.

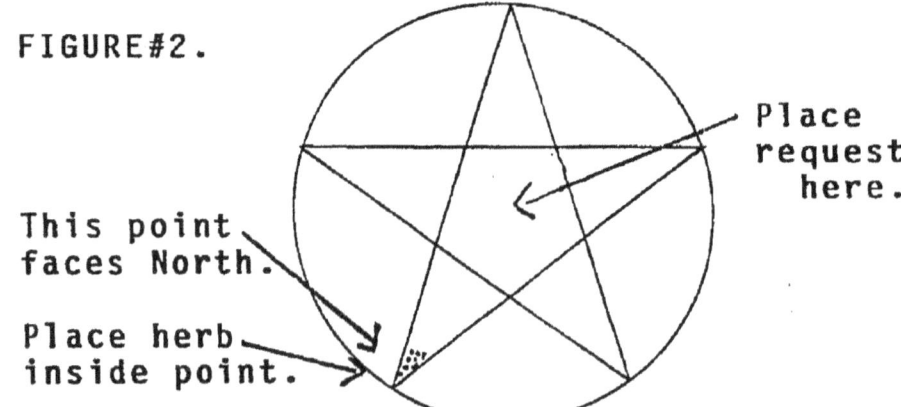

The best time to perform this particular ritual for gain in material matters, is during the time when the Moon is increasing towards full. Consult your calendar or almanac on this. The best time of the day is when you will not be disturbed.

When you have finished all preparations according to my instructions, repeat the following words in a soft but firm voice.

"PENTAGRAM, O STAR SO BRIGHT,
GRANT TO ME MAGICK MIGHT.
FULFILL MY WISH, SUPPLY MY NEED,
FOR AS I WILL, SO MOTE IT BE!"

When you have finished speaking, think strongly of your desire. Then, prepare to speak your desire out loud, but just when you are about to speak it, stop yourself from speaking your desire out loud. This unusual finish is a powerful technique to translate your desire into an intense energy that works along cosmic lines.

When you are finished with this ritual, burn the slip of paper, then mix the ashes with the Vervain herb and place it on your right hand. Go outside and blow it off your hand towards the North. Keep the Pentagramagick Energizer, which you have colored green in a secret place until you need to use for another ritual of this type. When you have used it several times, and it becomes worn, use a fresh copy of the large Pentagram.

3. USING THE PENTAGRAM FOR EMOTIONAL NEEDS

When you wish to apply the Power of the Pentagram in matters of the heart, or those of an emotional nature, both constructive and destructive, take a Pentagramagick Energizer and color it red.

Figure #1. shows that the lower right hand point of the Pentagram is the Magickal Gate of Fire, for emotional matters. Place your Pentagramagick Energizer on a table, making sure that the lower right hand point is pointing to the South.

Write down your request in a few words on a small sheet of paper, and place (with writing visible) on the center of the Pentagramagick Energizer. Also place a small amount of Mandrake within the lower right hand point. See Figure #3.

FIGURE #3.

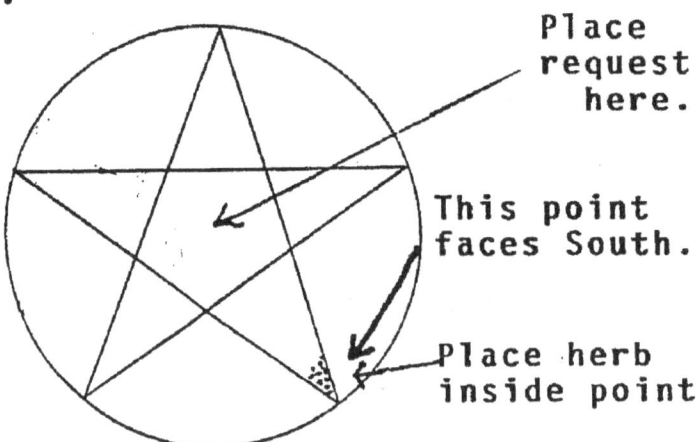

Place request here.

This point faces South.

Place herb inside point

Stand here facing the Pentagram

IMPORTANT!!!!!---When working rituals of the Fire Element (emotions), timing is important because this type of work can be used for either constructive or destructive purposes. The timing is related to the Moon: To gain something of an emotional nature, the best time would be as the Moon increases (between New and Full). To eliminate something of an emotional nature, the best time would be as the Moon decreases (after the Full Moon). For example, if you are working to bring a loving relationship into your life, you would ritual during the increase of the Moon. If you are trying to end such a relationship, then you would ritual during the decrease of the Moon. Another example is overcoming enemies: This should be done during the decrease of the Moon. Just remember, gaining or attracting during the increase of the Moon, fighting back or elimination during the decrease of the Moon.

When you have finished all preparations according to my instructions repeat the following words in a soft but firm voice.

"PENTAGRAM, O LIGHT SO DEAR,
IN YOUR LIGHT I NEVER FEAR.
FIRE WITHIN AND FIRE WITHOUT,
FROM MY SOUL I GIVE A SHOUT,
THAT ALL MAY HEED MY DECREE.
FOR AS I WILL, SO MOTE IT BE!"

When you have finished speaking, think strongly of your desire. Then, prepare to speak your desire out loud, but just when you are about to speak it, stop yourself from speaking your desire out loud. This unusual finish is a powerful technique to translate your desire into an intense energy that works along cosmic lines.

When you are finished with this ritual, burn the slip of paper, then mix the ashes with the Mandrake and place it in your right hand. Go outside and blow it off your hand towards the South. Keep the Pentagramagick Energizer, which you have colored red, in a secret place until you need to use it for another ritual of this type. When you have used it several times and it becomes worn, use a fresh copy of the large Pentagram.

4. USING THE PENTAGRAM FOR MORE MIND POWER

When you wish to apply the Power of the Pentagram in matters of mind such as, clear thinking, passing exams, mastering the study of any subject, etc., take a Pentagramagick Energizer and color it yellow.

Figure #1. shows that the upper left hand point of the Pentagram is the Magickal Gate of Air, for mental matters. Place your Pentagramagick Energizer on a table, making sure that the upper left hand point is pointing to the East.

Write down your request in a few words on a small sheet of paper, and place it (with writing visible) on the center of the Pentagramagick Energizer. Also place a small amount of Goldenrod within the upper left hand point. See Figure #4.

FIGURE #4

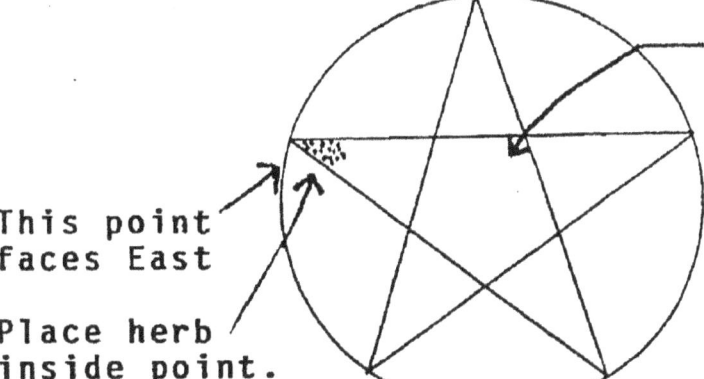

Place request here

This point faces East

Place herb inside point.

Stand here facing the Pentagram.

81

The best time to perform this ritual for gaining more mind power is during the increase of the Moon (between New and Full). When you have finished all preparations according to my instructions, repeat the following words in a soft but firm voice.

"PENTAGRAM, O STAR SO FAIR,
QUICKENING POWER OF THE AIR.
MAKE MY THOUGHTS REALITY,
FOR AS I WILL, SO MOTE IT BE!"

When you have finished speaking, think strongly of your desire. Then, prepare to speak your desire out loud, but just when you are about to speak it, stop yourself from speaking your desire out loud. This unusual finish is a powerful technique to translate your desire into an intense energy that works along cosmic lines.

When you are finished with this ritual, burn the slip of paper, then mix the ashes with the Goldenrod and place it in your right hand. Go outside and blow it off your hand towards the East. Keep the Pentagramagick Energizer, which you have colored yellow, in a secret place until you need to use it for another ritual of this type. When you have used it several times and it becomes worn, use a fresh copy of the large Pentagram.

5. USING THE PENTAGRAM FOR HEALING THE WHOLE PERSON

When you wish to apply the Power of the Pentagram in matters of healing, peace of mind, the harmonious blending of thought and emotion, obtaining guidance from the Land of Spirit, etc., take a Pentagramagick Energizer and color it blue.

Figure #1. shows that the upper right hand point of the Pentagram is the Magickal Gate of Water. Place your Pentagramagick Energizer on a table, making sure that the upper right hand point is pointing to the West.

Write down your request in a few words on a small sheet of paper, and place it (with writing visible) on the center of the Pentagramagick Energizer. Also place a small amount of Irish Moss within the upper right hand point. See Figure #5.

FIGURE #5.

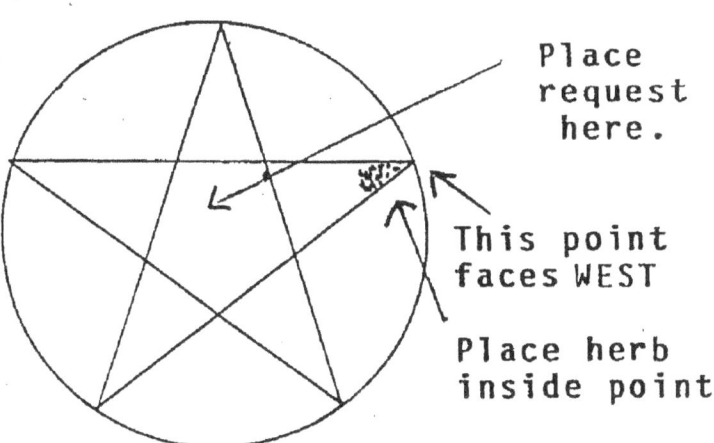

Place request here.

This point faces WEST

Place herb inside point

Stand here facing the Pentagram.

The best time to perform this type of ritual depends on what your purpose is. If you wish to eliminate a problem in the areas of life associated with this Magickal Gate, then the best time would be during the decrease of the Moon (after the Full Moon). But if your purpose is to gain something associated with this Magickal Gate, then the best time would be during the increase of the Moon (from New to Full). When you have finished all the preparations according to my instructions, repeat the following words in a soft but firm voice.

"PENTAGRAM, STAR OF PEACE.
LET ALL TURMOIL EVER CEASE.
LET MY ANSWER FLOW TO ME,
FOR AS I WILL, SO MOTE IT BE!"

When you have finished speaking, think strongly of your desire. Then, prepare to speak your desire out loud, but just when you are about to speak it, stop yourself from speaking your desire out loud. This unusual finish is a powerful technique to translate your desire into an intense energy that works along cosmic lines.

When you are finished with this ritual, burn the slip of paper, then mix the ashes with the Irish Moss and place it on your right hand. Go outside and blow it off your hand towards the West. Keep the Pentagramagick Energizer, which you have colored blue, in a secret place until you need to use it for another ritual of this type. When you have used it several times and it becomes worn, use a fresh copy of the large Pentagram.

6. ADVANCED TECHNIQUES OF PENTAGRAMAGICK

In this section of the booklet, I will reveal how you may apply the Power of the Pentagram for spiritual development, and an advanced technique to achieve and maintain balance and harmony in all areas of you life.

First, take a Pentagramagick Energizer, but do not color it. Figure #1. shows that the top single point of the Pentagram is the Magickal Gate of Ether (Spirit). Place your Pentagramagick Energizer on a table, making sure that the top single point is pointing to the East.

Write down your request in a few words on a small sheet of paper, and place it (with writing visible) on the center of the Pentagramagick Energizer. Also place a crystal within the top single point. See Figure #6.

FIGURE #6.

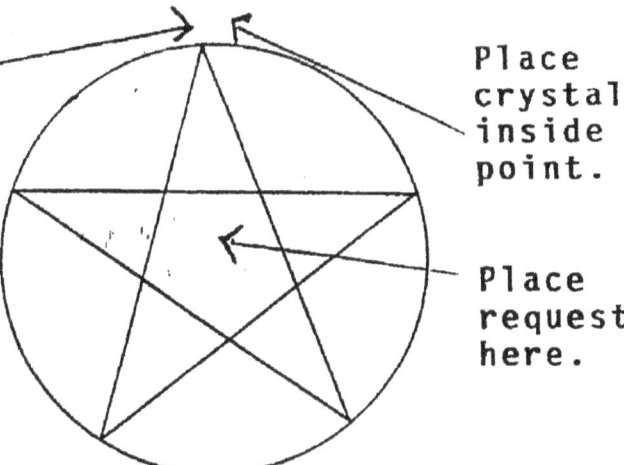

This point faces East.

Place crystal inside point.

Place request here.

Stand here facing the Pentagram.

This ritual may be performed any time of the month, because you will be linking with the Supreme Power, Universal Mind, God/Goddess, for whatever help or blessing you need. You will be attempting to become more aware of your Higher Self and the Ultimate Reality. Therefore, your request, when performing this ritual, should be related to discovering your highest spiritual potential, and achieving Divine Harmony at all levels of your being. When you are finished all preparations according to my instructions, repeat the following words in a soft but firm voice.

"PENTAGRAM, O GUIDING LIGHT,
LEAD ME TO THE INNER CHRIST.
MAY ALL OF ME BE IN HARMONY,
FOR AS I WILL, SO MOTE IT BE!"

When you have finished speaking, think strongly of your desire. Then, prepare to speak your desire out loud, but just as you are about to speak it, stop yourself from speaking your desire out loud. This unusual finish is a powerful technique to translate your desire into an intense energy that works along cosmic lines. In this particular ritual, there is an added power because of its spiritual nature.

When you are finished with this ritual, burn the slip of paper, then place the ashes on your right hand. Go outside and blow it off your hand towards the East. Keep the Pentagramagick Energizer in a secret place until you need to use it for another ritual of this type. When you have used it several times and it becomes worn, use a fresh copy of the large Pentagram. This particular ritual should be performed once or twice

a month.

The crystal that you use in this ritual may be used everyday for a special practice (or as often as you like). Keep this crystal and use it each time you perform this particular ritual. But you can also use it between sessions, as follows.

First, lie down on your back and place the crystal on your forehead. Spread your arms and legs, so as to form a human Pentagram. Just relax for as long as you like. You should will that the Ultimate Cosmic Energies channel through you, bringing balance, harmony and great power to you.

7. CLOSING THOUGHTS

How often should a practitioner use these Pentagram Rituals? The first four may be used whenever the practitioner feels the need to do so for a specific need in life. The fifth exercise should be performed once or twice a month. However, the crystal used in the fifth exercise may be used everyday, as described in the sixth or advanced technique.

Regardless of which exercise you are performing, follow these simply rules to assure greater success. First, when you complete a session, do not think too much about your desire. Release it to the Cosmos. This is done by doing everyday things until your next session. Second, when performing your work, put your heart into it. Use attention and feeling. Finally, be aware of opportunities that arise in your daily life that will guide you to the materialization of your desires, and take full advantage of each opportunity that comes your way. Remember this rule always, "Do what you will as long as it harms none".

What is Pentagramagick?

You will learn a system of using the pentagram mixed with other elements to manifest your desires, safely, quickly and easily. This method was given to the author on the inner planes of wisdom and has not been revealed before.

The Pentagram
(Why is this symbol called evil?)

In this booklet you will find out why certain groups and individuals want you to fear this symbol.

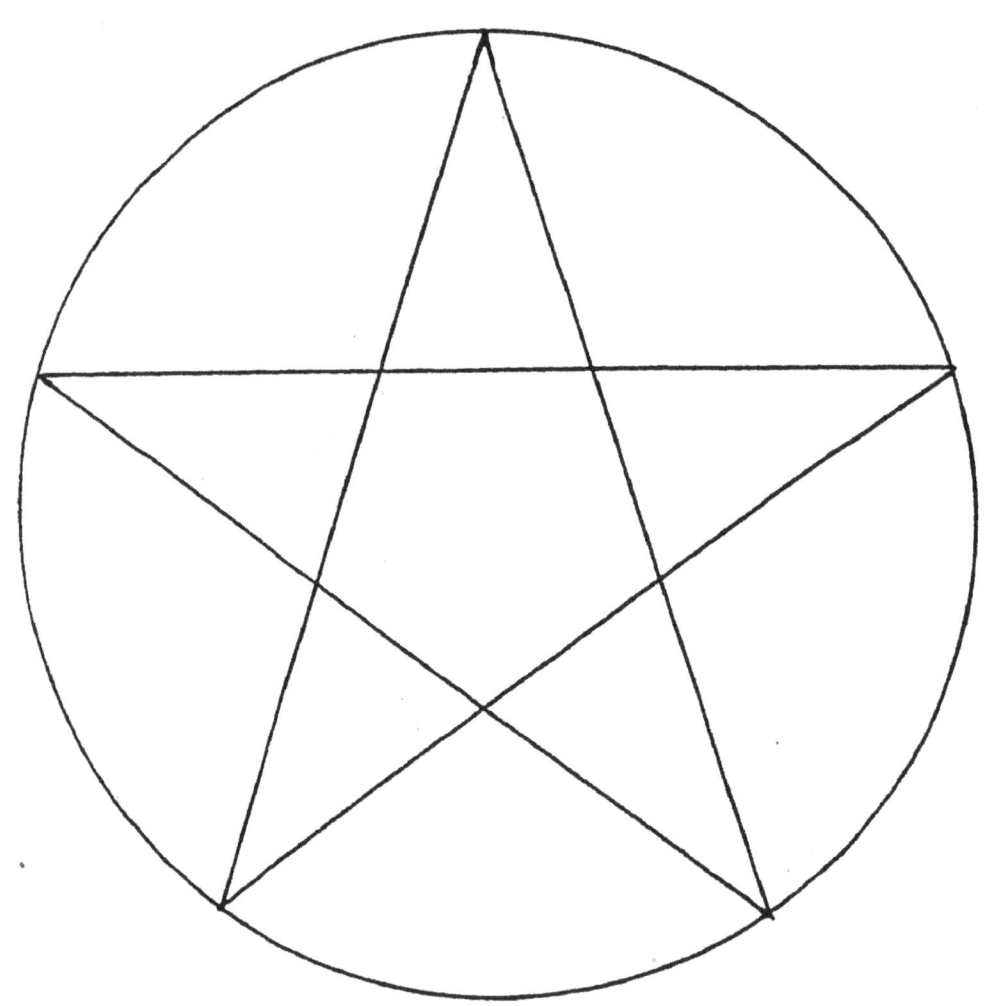

90

INNER LIGHT PUBLICATIONS

Since 1965, William Alexander Oribello taught thousands of people how to improve their lives in every way, through the proper applications of mystical sciences.

If you would like more information about other books by William Oribello, please write to:

Inner Light Publications
P.O. Box 753
New Brunswick, NJ 08903

www.ingramcontent.com/pod-product-compliance
Lightning Source LLC
Chambersburg PA
CBHW080523110426
42742CB00017B/3214